TO

DAVID

WITH SINCERE APPRECIATION

AND BEST WISHES.

Christopher Oyesiku
Jan. 2017

CHRISTOPHER OYESIKU

Preeminent Nigerian Choral Conductor

GODWIN SADOH
BESTSELLING AUTHOR ON AMAZON

iUniverse, Inc.
Bloomington

Christopher Oyesiku
Preeminent Nigerian Choral Conductor

iUniverse books may be ordered through booksellers or by contacting:

iUniverse
1663 Liberty Drive
Bloomington, IN 47403
www.iuniverse.com
1-800-Authors (1-800-288-4677)

ISBN: 978-1-4502-9109-5 (sc)
ISBN: 978-1-4502-9110-1 (ebk)

Printed in the United States of America

iUniverse rev. date: 01/25/2011

Contents

Acknowledgments

I deeply express utmost gratitude to Christopher Oyesiku for providing me with all the relevant documents, concert programs, newspaper reviews, and personal photos for writing this book to preserve his contribution to Nigerian music and his legacy for present and future generations. More importantly, words cannot articulate my sincere appreciation to Oyesiku for answering every single question I asked him about his life and astonishing musical career that spanned over six decades. For the first time in my writing career, I wrote two books in two continents, two countries, and five states. These countries are Nigeria and the United States—Alabama, Tennessee, Kentucky, Indiana, and Ohio. For this type of roving laboratory, I coined the concept "intellectual caravan." I define "intellectual caravan" as a fieldwork that entails the collection of data, transcription, analysis, and the writing of a book or essay derived from the collectanea[1] on the road and/or across several states, countries, or continents. In other words, the book is researched and completely written on the road as the scholar collects the data. Therefore, I am truly indebted to all the libraries that allowed me to use

---

1   Folklorists refer to all the things a fieldworker labeled and put into pockets or boxes or the trunk of the car as "collectanea." The category includes tapes, notes, films, and drawings. See Bruce Jackson, *Fieldwork* (Urbana and Chicago: University of Illinois Press, 1987), 7.

their facilities including the public libraries of Jackson and Nashville in Tennessee, Louisville in Kentucky, Indianapolis in Indiana, as well as the Columbus Metropolitan Library, Saint John Learning Center in Columbus, Ohio, and Saint Andrews Anglican Church at Lewis Center in Ohio.

Preface

This book is specially written as a tribute to recognize life-work accomplishments of Christopher Valentine Olakanmi Oyesiku, foremost Nigerian classical bass singer, choral conductor extraordinaire, music educator, erudite scholar, concert promoter, concert manager, concert connoisseur, and broadcaster. Christopher Oyesiku is highly esteemed among a selected group of professionally trained Nigerians who vigorously and painstakingly nurtured and preserved classical music tradition in Nigeria. His contributions spanning over six decades to the growth and development of classical music in Nigeria are 'priceless.' He fostered the music through teaching in Nigerian higher institutions, through broadcasting on radio waves, through exquisite choral training and conducting, through presentation of scholarly papers at international conferences around the world, by organizing numerous breadth-taking concerts of vocal and instrumental genres, and by singing bass solo himself, from standard repertoire of famous European, American, and modern Nigerian composers. For all these trailblazing, exceptional, flamboyant, and gargantuan achievements, Christopher Oyesiku is honored with this tome. This book is divided into five chapters: Chapter 1 presents a brief account of classical music performance in Nigeria from late nineteenth century to present time; chapter 2 relays a short biography of Christopher Oyesiku; chapters 3 and 4 present a selection of succinct newspaper reviews of Christopher Oyesiku's solo and choral concerts from 1960 to 1995; chapter 5 is a summation of the eulogies bestowed on Christopher Oyesiku by his friends, colleagues, dignitaries, and admirers.

Chapter 1

Introduction

When the missionaries from Europe and the United States arrived in Nigeria around mid-nineteenth century with their Bibles and hymn books, little did they know of how their activities would create a profound change to the musical landscape and life style in the most populous African nation. The missionaries' dogma in collaboration with the colonial educational policies soon filtered into the society, resultant products of new musical styles, genres, instruments, performing centers, performing styles, languages, dressing, etiquettes, singing techniques, and repertoire. Classical music introduced to Nigerians was both sacred and secular. Sacred works were mostly confined to worship in the Christian church, while secular music was performed in concert halls. However, large sacred works such as cantatas and oratorios were included in programs of public concerts.

The taste for classical music emanating from colonization and missionary exercises, invariably contributed to the stratification of Nigerian society into three main socio-economic groups: the lower class, upper-middle-class, and the affluent. The lower class consists of the poor and uneducated Nigerians at the grass root level. The upper-middle-class is the elite and well-educated indigenes; while the affluent is made up of the rich and powerful citizens. Similar to the cultural experience in American and European countries, classical music followership in Nigeria belongs to a small segment of the society, primarily, the upper-middle-class and affluent groups. Art music is patronized and disseminated by these two special groups in Nigeria. This should not be surprising because classical music is only taught at churches, schools, and privately at the homes of the bourgeoisie. It is also important to stress that classical music is only found within the Christian circles in Nigeria; therefore, its composers, performers and audiences are all Christians. The reason for this is not far-fetched because art music emanated from the Christian church, and mission and colonial schools in Nigeria. That is why it is still confined to the Christian arena in the country.

The introduction of classical music to Nigeria also brought about cultural assimilation and acculturation; in today's dictum, interculturalism. One could perceive intercultural phenomenon in the total fabric of Nigerian art music from various angles, such as the use of English and indigenous languages as texts in the music, and the spoken addresses by the Master of Ceremony or compere at the beginning, intermission, and at the end of the concert; the costumes of the artists and choirs as well as the dresses of the audiences that are usually in both English and traditional attires; accompaniment of the music consisting of Western and Nigerian traditional instruments; the concert venues, that are normally a church, concert hall or a theater—the sacred and the mundane; Nigerians performing music from other cultures; Nigerian composers writing Western classical music; and the non-participatory experience of the audience in the concert except for the delayed and well-coordinated applause expected at the end of each performance. All these factors clearly delineate the musical practice in Nigeria as intercultural.

Unlike my previous books that investigate the process of composition and ethnomusicology in Nigeria; this book succinctly introduces musicians and enthusiasts to the performance of classical music in

Nigeria through the life and stunning career of Christopher Oyesiku. His repertoire, bass solo recitals and choral performances are indeed the epitome of art music concerts in Nigeria. In this book, we can see how art music is taught and learned, organized, directed, performed, promoted, managed, disseminated, patronized, and preserved by the elitist group in modern day Nigeria. In other words, the Christopher Oyesiku concerts are representative of art music decorum in Nigeria, with particular emphasis on the performance practices, and a mirror through which one could examine the ethos of this brand of music in twenty-first century Nigeria.

Chapter 2

The Biography of Christopher Oyesiku

Christopher Valentine Olakanmi Oyesiku was born in Lagos, Nigeria, on 7 October, 1925. His father was Ladipo Oyesiku, a chemist. His grandfather was Chief Charles Valentine Oyekanmi Oyesiku, the Aseru of Erunwon and Baye of Oba in Abeokuta, Ogun State. Coming from the Well-known Taylor family, the late Chief changed his name to Oyesiku on assuming his chieftaincy titles. Oyesiku's mother was Victoria Oyesiku, a well-loved teacher at Saint John's Primary School, Aroloya, Lagos; her father, a teacher at CMS Grammar School, Lagos, was Simeon Dina Pratt, who later became a Court Registrar in Lagos.

Formative Years in Lagos

Oyesiku began his secondary school education in Lagos at Saint John's Primary School, Aroloya, and at CMS Grammar School, but completed it at the Ibadan Grammar School in 1947. It was around 1933 that Oyesiku began his earliest musical training as a choir-boy at the Anglican Cathedral Church of Christ, Lagos, under the tutelage of Thomas Ekundayo Phillips (1884-1969). It was Phillips who gave the young Oyesiku his first music lessons in the theory of music, musicianship, and voice. Phillips also coached the young Oyesiku for the external examinations of the Trinity College of Music, London.

Cathedral Church of Christ, Lagos.

Thomas Ekundayo Phillips.

While Oyesiku was a choir member, he was fortunate to move closely with the late Archbishop Leslie Gordon Vining (1885-1955), bishop of Lagos, from 1940 to 1955. He became the first Archbishop of the newly inaugurated Province of West Africa, Anglican Communion, in 1951, a position he held until his demise in 1955. He was the last bishop of Lagos of European descent. This remarkable man of God was humble and holy, one of the great divines of the twentieth century. Archbishop Vining sought out the best from everybody and turned no one away from his door. His religious mission was exemplary and he was a challenge and a model to all who came in contact with him. All the choristers, members of the congregation, and other priests in the diocese loved him. Vining was a source of inspiration to Christians and non-Christians as well. Archbishop Vining ran a boys' camp during the school holidays at *Kuramo* Waters in Lagos. Oyesiku was privileged to be quartermaster of the camp. At the camp, the boys worked together as a team. Oyesiku was a strong swimmer, thus, he taught many of the boys how to swim. Memorable were the huge camp fires and the humorous readings of the bishop's camp log on Saturday evenings, followed by a celebration of the Holy Communion on Sunday mornings in the open air chapel by the lagoon. These bodacious events all took place under a simple hanging cross, surrounded by coconut palm trees.

During his time as chorister at the Cathedral Church, Oyesiku rose to become one of the leading trebles and later became the best bass in the choir. As his voice deepened, he became a lay clerk under the eminent Nigerian Organist and Master of the Music, Thomas Ekundayo Phillips,[2] and remained a member of the choir until he left to study music in Great Britain in 1955. Oyesiku joined the Lagos Musical Society in the late 1940s and took part as a leading bass soloist in Gilbert and Sullivan's comic operas such as the *Trial by Jury, HMS Pinafore* and the *Mikado.* Oyesiku also sang the part of Elijah in the Mendelssohn's

---

2 Thomas Ekundayo Phillips was Organist and Master of the Music at the Cathedral Church of Christ, Lagos, from Trinity Sunday 1914 to Trinity Sunday 1962.

Elijah, a work that has become one of his favorite oratorios. His last performance in the *Elijah* was in April 1985 at the Cathedral Church of Christ, Lagos. Oyesiku won the silver medal in singing at the Festival of Arts Competition at Lagos, in the late 1940s and early 1950s. The festival was created by a group of eminent personalities among who were the late Major J. G. C. Allen (a British colonial administrator who later became the Director of Administration at the Nigerian Broadcasting Corporation) and Tunji Adeniyi Jones.

After graduating high school, Oyesiku was apprenticed to the Nigerian Railway Printing Press on 1 April, 1948. At this company, he was taught the rudiments of printing for two years. This provided an excellent foundation for his future career, evidenced in his ability to ensure a top-notch quality of the printing of his music programs. In 1950, he joined the Social Welfare Department in Lagos as a Probation Officer. This gave him a clear and deep insight into the behavioral patterns of human kind, in particular, concerning the relationship of parents and guardians to their children and wards. In 1952, Oyesiku joined the staff of the Nigerian Broadcasting Corporation (now Federal Radio Corporation of Nigeria) and three years later he was awarded a Federal Government Scholarship to study music at the Guildhall School of Music and Drama, London.

Musical Training in England

Oyesiku arrived in England to study music in 1955 and his voice teacher was Ellis Keeler. Oyesiku's wife, Femi Oyesiku, comes from the Iporo Ake Coker family of Abeokuta. They married on 14 April, 1956, at Saint Albans Church, Westbury Park, Bristol. This was the church where Archbishop Vining was priest from 1918 to 1938, before being consecrated as bishop of Lagos. Oyesiku and his wife are blessed with two children. While in England, Oyesiku took part as a soloist in several secular and sacred concerts, two of which were very memorable: The Commonwealth Gala Concert in May 1958, in the presence of HRH Princess Alice, Countess of Athlone; and a concert of Three

Bach Cantatas in Sherborne Abbey, in December 1958. This concert was conducted by Paul Steinitz. Oyesiku was also the leading bass at St. Michael's Church, Chester Square, London, where Sir Arthur Sullivan of the Gilbert and Sullivan duo was organist from 1861 to 1872. Oyesiku made his debut on BBC Television on 19 June, 1960, having passed the required singing auditions. He took part in various programs for the BBC overseas services as well. At the end of five years of studies and career accomplishments in England, Oyesiku earned several diplomas of music:

1. Associate of the Guildhall School of Music in Teaching (1958).
2. Associate of the Guildhall School of Music in Singing Performance (1959).
3. Licentiate of the Royal Academy of Music in Singing Performance (1959).
4. Licentiate of the Trinity College of Music (1959).
5. Teacher Training Certificate of Music, Guildhall School of Music (1959).
6. Fellowship of the Trinity College of Music (1960).

**Christopher and Femi Oyesiku's Wedding at
Saint Albans Church, Bristol, 1956.**

Christopher and Femi Oyesiku's Wedding at Saint Albans Church, Bristol, 1956.

Other prominent Nigerian professional musicians who studied at the Guildhall School of Music included James Adekunle, the first Director of the School of Music, of the Music Society of Nigeria (MUSON), Lagos; Ayo Bankole (1935-1976); Tolu Obajimi, Organist and Master of the Music, Cathedral Church of Christ, Lagos; Kehinde Okusanya, Controller of Music, Federal Radio Corporation of Nigeria; Cecilia Odiah, Nigerian soprano; Sola Abayomi of the Nigerian Police Band; and Joshua Uzoigwe (1946-2005).

Professional Career in Nigeria

On his return to Nigeria in 1960, Oyesiku introduced the first analytical programs of Nigerian music on Radio Nigeria, western region, Ibadan, and commenced his life long career of choral training and conducting for recording purposes. He also participated as soloist in performances at the University College Ibadan (now University of Ibadan). He was called on to act as a judge at the 1961 Festival of the Arts competitions in the western region and donated a cup for the best solo singer. In addition to his accomplishment as a fine bass singer, Oyesiku has earned a reputation in Nigeria as a distinguished choral conductor, as well as an astonishing choir trainer.

When he was transferred to Lagos in 1962, Oyesiku took over the Nigerian Broadcasting Corporation Choir and trained it to a level of such excellence that it was widely acclaimed for its rendering of both secular and sacred music. At Lagos, he became the first Controller of Music of the Federal Radio Corporation of Nigeria. As Head of Music and Music Research, Controller of Music and Assistant Director of Programs in Radio Nigeria, Oyesiku carried out various administrative and program duties, such as the recruitment, promotion, discipline of staff, the allocation of apartments, the preparation of estimates (budgets) and control of expenditure in the departments under him. He presented weekly programs and recorded Christian services for broadcast every week using the NBC Choir in many of them. Bellow is a synopsis of some of the programs created and produced by Oyesiku while in the service of the Nigerian Broadcasting Corporation.

**Christopher Oyesiku at the Nigerian
Broadcasting Corporation in the 1970s.**

Programs at the Nigerian Broadcasting Corporation

While at the service of the Nigerian Broadcasting Corporation, Oyesiku produced several programs and had this to say: "As I look back on the period of almost thirty years that I spent in the Nigerian Radio establishment, I feel deeply gratified at my achievements in the numerous music programs that I compiled, created, produced, and personally presented. Out of these, I have selected the few that I was most delighted and satisfied with."

Concert Hour

This weekly program was one of the oldest music programs on radio Nigeria. It was broadcast on Sundays, with a repeat on Wednesdays. Oyesiku inherited it in 1952 and handed it over to Clara Akinsemoyin in 1981. In those days, there were no secretaries and the scripts had to be handwritten with a carbon copy every week. It comprised international classical music and was greatly enjoyed by all lovers of classical music in Nigeria. Nigerian composers were also included. One of the important music Oyesiku had the honor of broadcasting from Ibadan, was that of a concert given by Fela Sowande at the Carnegie Hall, in the United States; that was a historic occasion. His works were performed by the New York Philharmonic Orchestra and was conducted by Fela Sowande himself. The two hour recording was sent to Oyesiku by the United States Information Service in Ibadan, Nigeria. The program was compered[3] by Joe Atuana, one of Nigeria's most accomplished broadcasters. The program included Sowande's *Folk Symphony,* specially composed for Nigerian Independence in 1960.

Meet the Artists

This was a weekly fifteen minute program that Oyesiku created and presented. It ran for over ten years from 1965 to 1978. The program featured Nigerian and international artists of different musical skills

---

3   Compere is a British phrase for Master of Ceremony.

and virtuosity. They performed mainly international music but included Nigerian art music when available. The artists were introduced to the Nigerian listeners through their recordings and when possible, live performances.

Victoria de Los Angeles – Soprano

Elizabeth Schwarzkopf – Soprano

Akin Euba – Piano

Vladimir Horowitz – Piano

Dinu Lipatti – Piano

Margaret Evans – Piano

Richard Lewis – Tenor

Boris Christoff – Bass

Norman Walker – Bass

Fela Sowande – Organ

Olaolu Omideyi – Organ

Charles Oluwole Obayomi Phillips[4] – Organ

Albert Schweitzer – Organ

Christopher Oyesiku – Bass

These were a few of the artists whose programs were stimulating and exciting. Visiting artists, who were invited by embassies or their cultural institutes, were often recorded and included in the series.

4   Charles Oluwole Obayomi Phillips succeeded his father, Thomas Ekundayo Phillips, as Organist and Master of the Music, at the Cathedral Church of Christ, Lagos, from Trinity Sunday 1962 to Trinity Sunday 1992.

Choral Singing

This was one of the most popular and cherished music programs that catered to the Nigerians natural love for singing. They listened enthusiastically to enjoy the programs and learn from them. The programs were aimed at improving the standard of singing through radio. Oyesiku presented the series and featured national and international choirs of excellent standard. Nigerian church choirs and other choral groups were invited to participate. Before recordings, Oyesiku would visit the choirs at least twice to help train them in the techniques of breathing, good intonation, blending of voices, balance, and presentation of their programs to improve the quality of their performances. These helped enormously with the final production of each program. Many choral groups wrote to request inclusion in the series.

Music of the Masters/Meet the Composers

This series that Oyesiku introduced in 1965 and produced by himself ran initially for six months. It was a series on the music of the great masters presented by Nigerian professional musicians. The duration was thirty minutes in which the presenter discussed the life and compositions of a particular composer, for instance, Handel. Although, introduced initially for six months, it kept being included in the schedules because of the inexhaustible nature of the musical personalities and materials. It practically became an annual program.

Traditional Music

Various music programs illustrated and presented music of traditional rulers like the Obas (kings) and chiefs of the south, the Emirs (kings) of the north, and the Obis (Kings) and Obongs (Kings) of the east. The music in these programs expressed the pomp and dignity of the courts of the rulers; for example, the Shehu of Borno's personal band or the drumming in the courts of Yoruba Obas. Particular programs in which the music of Nigerian rulers including that of the isolated islands of the Delta, have been presented are:

1. Drums and Voices
2. Our Kind of Music
3. Our Musical Heritage
4. Yoruba Music and Customs

The program, Our Musical Heritage, presented serious traditional music. Various pieces of music were analyzed, including full descriptions of the instruments used, the occasion on which the music was played, and the historical background of the music. The program, Yoruba Music and Customs, introduced by Oyesiku, was a series presented by the local rulers. The first eminent ruler/musician was the Timi of Ede, Oba Adetoyese Laoye I. The program series provided a unique opportunity for obtaining good and genuine indigenous music, and was planned to extend to other part of the country. The last program Oyesiku initiated and produced was Guide to Nigerian Music. This series was presented by Nigerian composers of art music. Presenters included Wilberforce Echezona, Akin Euba, Lazarus Ekwueme, and Ayo Bankole. In the series, they explained and analyzed various types of Nigerian music, describing fully the origin, purpose, and form of the music. They also explained the vocal techniques of the singers and the structures of the musical instruments.

Choral Conducting Career

In addition to his seamless duties at the Nigerian Broadcasting Corporation, Oyesiku became the Director of Music of the Lagos Musical Society Choir that was popular for its triennial concerts and the Nigerian Broadcasting Corporation Choir. He conducted both choirs from 1963 to 1981. The NBC Choir, apart from singing weekly services and taking part regularly in concerts, presented several command performances for former Heads of State, including Generals Yakubu Gowon and Olusegun Obasanjo, at the Head of State's residence, Dodan Barracks, Lagos. These performances usually took place during the Easter and Christmas seasons. Oyesiku's Service of Nine Lessons and

Carols held on December 24 annually, was so popular that even though it was always a live broadcast, the venue, Saint Peter's Anglican Church, Faji, was often packed full thirty minutes prior to the commencement of the service. Obviously, with all these accolades, Oyesiku was convinced that the NBC Choir fulfilled the purpose for which it was founded, that is, to set a high standard of singing in both secular and church music. His choir work was in addition to his duties as a producer. Oyesiku also trained and conducted the choirs that sang the Games' Anthem, *Mighty Africa,* composed by Ayo Bankole during the All Africa Games in 1973, and the *FESTAC* anthem during the All Africa Festival of Black Arts and Culture in 1977. In 1979, Oyesiku coordinated the selection of the current Nigerian National Anthem and trained the choir that made the official version recording.

Solo Career

Running parallel with all these extremely hectic schedule was Oyesiku's solo career at several concerts including the NBC Cultural Nights, embassy concerts, and other high profiled events organized in Lagos, Ibadan, Nsukka, and even as far as other West African countries such as Ghana and Cameroon. Indeed, Oyesiku was divinely blessed with a magnificent bass voice unparalleled to none before or after him in Nigeria and the whole of the African continent. The Ghanaian *Daily Graphic* had this to say of him in May 1967 when he performed in Accra: "Christopher Oyesiku's voice, to my mind, should be for the world. Nigeria is certainly very fortunate to have the joy and pleasure of it in their midst." One of the highlights of his career was the invitation from Sir David Willcocks to sing at Saint Jude's Anglican Church, Ebute-Metta, Nigeria, in a solo part of the Carol, *The Three Kings.* In this elite performance, Oyesiku sang with the choir of King's College, Cambridge, conducted by Willcocks himself, during their visit to Lagos in 1972. On two occasions in 1972 and 1979, he served as one of the judges at the BBC's world-wide choral competition, "Let the People Sing." He retired from Radio Nigeria as Assistant Director of Programs in 1981.

Christopher Oyesiku Sings Solo in *Three Kings* with
King's College Choir, 1972.

Christoper Oyesiku.

International Scholarly Contribution

Oyesiku also represented the Nigerian Broadcasting Corporation at various international conferences. These included the African Music Rostrum meetings in Venice in 1973, and Ghana in 1976; the International Music Center Congress (IMZ) in Salzburg in August 1974, where he read a paper on "Music and Radio in African Countries;" Oyesiku also contributed to the discussion on "Music and Tomorrow's Public;" he attended the IMZ world's Congresses in Toronto in 1975 and in Vienna in August 1977, where he read the paper entitled, "Dissemination of Music and Culture through radio and Record in Nigeria." Oyesiku was appointed a member of the Executive Board of IMZ in October 1977. After the African Rostrum meeting, the Music Counselor from Egypt wrote in a letter dated 9 September, 1973, to the Director General of NBC: "I took the occasion of the second African Music Rostrum to write to you expressing my pleasure at meeting the representative of the Nigerian Broadcasting Corporation, Christopher Oyesiku. As a member of the selection committee, his contribution was outstanding. I admired so much his personality, his logic, strong, honest and straight forward arguments, and very polite manners."

On his retirement from the Nigerian Broadcasting Corporation, Oyesiku received the following approbation from Sunday Young Harry, Zonal Director, Lagos:

> May I take this opportunity to express my appreciation for the enormous contribution you have made to broadcasting in the twenty-nine years of your meritorious service. Indeed, you have been amongst the longest serving members of staff of the Corporation and your hard work, loyalty, and dedication, over the years are amply documented in your records. In a career spanning three decades, it would be invidious to single out a particular area in which your influence was most prominent; but one cannot lose sight of your highly commendable leadership role in the Music Department of the Corporation and your drive and competence. The FRCN Choir has brought the

Corporation considerable pride in their many performances on state occasions and in other churches throughout the country. You, as director, have every right to derive utmost satisfaction from these enviable achievements.

Teaching Career

Oyesiku retired from the Nigerian Broadcasting Corporation as the Assistant Director of Programs in 1981. Between 1982 and 1987, Oyesiku was the Chair of the Department of Music, Oyo State College of Education, Ilesha. As the head of the music program, his *mantra* was to train the future breed of excellent Nigerian musicians. The educational standard set by Oyesiku was so high that all the students who obtained the requisite Ordinary Level diploma[5] at the college were admitted to the bachelor's music program at the University of Ife (now Obafemi Awolowo University, Ile-Ife). While in Ilesha, he organized a high-class choir that performed concerts regularly on campus and surrounding vicinity of the institution. The college choir was well known for its annual Festival of Lessons and Carols during the Christmas season. These concerts usually attracted elite audiences from various parts of southwest Nigeria, including music lecturers from the Obafemi Awolowo University, Ile-Ife, and the University of Ibadan. In June 1985, Oyesiku was invited by the Nigerian-British Association to take part in a celebrity concert in London in the presence of HRH Princess Alexandra of England.

In 1987, Oyesiku was officially invited to the University of Ibadan as an Artist-in-Residence, by the then Vice-Chancellor, Professor Ayo Banjo, to revitalize the musical life of the institution and to develop a reputable choir for the institution. As the Artist-in-Residence for ten years (1987-1997), Oyesiku did fulfilled the expectations of the Vice-Chancellor and left an indelible mark in the form of the well-established university choir and a thriving audience for classical music who attended

---

5   The Nigerian Ordinary Level diploma is equivalent to the United States community college diploma.

most of the forty concerts he organized. His duties as Artist-in-Residence at the university included imparting the art of voice production to all the undergraduate students at the Department of Theatre Arts; and training the University Choir as well as organizing musical events for the entire university community including the musically inclined populace of the surrounding towns of Ibadan. In addition to participating in many of the concerts, the choir also performed regularly at Convocations (Commencements). The first major concert was that for the fortieth anniversary of the University of Ibadan on 12 November, 1988, where the university anthem was premiered. Professor Isidore Okpewho of the Department of English, University of Ibadan, wrote the words, while the music was composed by the Nigerian musician Olaolu Omideyi. The anthem was a significant part of the fortieth anniversary celebrations of the premier university in 1988. Oyesiku, as the Director of the University of Ibadan Choir and President of the Music Circle, University of Ibadan branch, organized, directed and took part in the following programs:

- Celebrity Concert in honor of the Nobel Prize Winner for Literature in 1986, Professor Wole Soyinka, on 7 March, 1987.
- The Inaugural Concert of the University of Ibadan Choir on 12 October, 1987.
- Concert to commemorate the Silver Jubilee Anniversary of the University of Ibadan, School of Drama and the Department of Theater Arts, at the Trenchard Hall, on Friday, 22 July, 1988.
- Youth Concert of Classical Music for the Children's International Summer Village, Nigeria, at the Trenchard Hall, University of Ibadan, on Wednesday, 17 August, 1988.
- Fortieth Anniversary Celebration Concert sponsored by ELF Nigeria Limited, at the Trenchard Hall, University of Ibadan, on Saturday, 12 November, 1988, in the presence of Professor

Ayo Banjo, the then Vice Chancellor of the University of Ibadan and Mrs. Alice Banjo.

To protract a continuous lofty standard, Oyesiku invited the best artists available, both Nigerians and foreigners to perform as soloists and accompanists at his concerts. These included Femi Akinkugbe, Funmilayo Boamah, Joy Nwosu Lo-Bamijoko – sopranos; Mosunmola Omibiyi Obidike – mezzo soprano; Lazarus Ekwueme – tenor; Michael Hudson and David Williams – baritones; Ajibola Meshida – violin; the ace trumpeter, Zeal Onyia; and the pianists – Godwin Sadoh, Christopher Ayodele, Ayo Bankole Jr., Emmanuel Boamah, Edward Boamah, Richard Bucknor, Thora Dubois, Amorelle Inanga, and Joyce Lowe. On 10 November, 1987, Oyesiku organized and took part in a recital given by a visiting British concert organist, Peter Stevenson. The recital was held at Saint Peter's Anglican Church, Aremo, Ibadan. He also helped the British Council in Nigeria to organize a jazz concert for the "Itchy Fingers" (a British jazz band) on 9 March, 1988. The concert took place at the Trenchard Hall, Ibadan. On 23 November, 1988, Oyesiku participated in the All Stars Night Concert to mark the seventieth Choir Festival of the Cathedral Church of Christ, Lagos.

Oyesiku's solo repertoire includes the following major works— Oratorios: *The Messiah, Creation, Elijah, Samson, Acis and Galatea, B Minor Mass, Judas Maccabeus, Stabat Mater,* and *Alexander's Feast;* operas: *The Magic Flute, The Marriage of Figaro, Don Carlos, Don Giovanni, Simon Boccanegra,* and *Der Freischutz.* His repertoire also includes *lieder* and songs of general interest. In both his singing and choral work, he gives special prominence to the compositions of Nigerians made available to him and that are of high standard.

Closing Remarks

Through out his musical career, Oyesiku has always encouraged his contemporaries by inviting them to take part in his concerts and by giving them credit for their accomplishments. In addition, he has taken many of the younger musicians to task, including the author of this book; trying to make them understand that it is only by persistence, hard work and dedication that one can achieve a high standard of performance. His ideals are lofty and his achievements no less. Oyesiku is very disturbed by the low standard of musical performance and musical training available generally in Nigeria, and the relegation to the background of qualified musicians. This he attributes to the lack of the practical teaching of music in the Departments of Music of higher institutions and the reluctance of trained musicians to work together for the furtherance of good music. Oyesiku has retired from active music career. He presently lives with his wife in London, England. Apart from music, Oyesiku has his lighter moments. His hobbies are swimming, reading, and in his younger days, dancing. He is deeply religious and enjoys worshipping in the Anglican tradition with good music.[6]

---

6   The biography of Christopher Oyesiku was derived from six personal interviews with him on 20 June, 1990; 15 March, 2007; 2 August, 2010; 22 September, 2010; 20 October, 2010; and 26 October, 2010.

Chapter 3

Solo Performances

Christopher Oyesiku dazzled the Nigerian elitist classical music caucuses with his extraordinary bass voice and God-gifted talent for well over six decades. His outstanding performances brought smiles, laughter, joy, and admiration to the faces of his faithful patrons, patronesses, and audiences. Nigeria has never seen nor heard anything like Oyesiku's magnificent voice that is best described as *bel canto* and *basso profundo*. With this rare voice, he always leaves an impeccable and memorable impression on his ardent *aficionados*. He has performed before the cream of Nigerian society, African nations, dignitaries, and indeed, the Royal Family in Great Britain. Below are excerpts from selected newspaper reviews of some of Oyesiku's brilliant solo performances in England and Nigeria.

Christopher Oyesiku, who was one of the first Nigerians to join the Nigerian Broadcasting Service in 1952, will be one of the first few Nigerians to appear on British television. He will make his debut on Sunday. After Oyesiku had been for a BBC television audition, the report on his card said, "An ideal Othello if only he were a tenor." He will sing on Sunday in the last program in the series "Music with Max," that features Max Jaffa and Trio. Oyesiku has appeared many times in

BBC sound programs, particularly in the General Overseas Programs, "Calling Nigeria" and "Calling West Africa." Oyesiku at twenty-nine years old commented: "I have learnt a great deal in England and I realize now how little I knew when I came here. I am going to fight for other Nigerians to come here to study and perfect their art, whatever it is. When I get back to work in the Lagos Musical Society, I hope to contribute to the development of music in Nigeria."[7] He certainly did, in a significant way.

---

7   *Daily Service,* Thursday, 16 June, 1960.

Christopher Oyesiku as foreman of the jury in
Gilbert and Sullivan's *Trial by Jury*, 1953

Christopher Oyesiku chatting with the Countess o
Athlone after performing at the Commonwealth Gala
Concert, on Thursday 8th May 1958

Christopher with Princess Alexandra of Kent after
a concert at Overseas House for the Victoria League
performed in St James', July 1959

Christopher sitting beside Bob Armstrong in a
photograph of the cast of Haydn's *Creatio*
in Ibadan, January 1961

Christopher Oyesiku in Concerts, 1950s-1960s.

The well-known bass singer, Christopher Oyesiku, made his first public appearance on Thursday, 26 January, 1960, in the Trenchard Hall, at the University College Ibadan (now University of Ibadan), when he sang in Haydn's oratorio, *Creation*. Oyesiku who returned from Britain in December 1959, after five years' study, was for the last five years before his departure in 1955, Nigeria's most popular and well-known bass singer, particularly where he sang for the Lagos Musical Society and in the Cathedral Church of Christ Choir, Lagos. In his appearance tonight and tomorrow, he will be singing in the University College Ibadan Music Circle and the Musical Society annual joint performance. Other soloists in the performance are Janetta Mayer (soprano), Jim Gardner (tenor), and Bob Armstrong (baritone). The choir and orchestra will be conducted by Peter Konstam. It is reported that arrangements are completed to take the performance of Haydn's *Creation* to Lagos on Saturday, 28 January, where it will take place in the Lagos Anglican Cathedral Church of Christ.[8]

---

8   *The University Observer,* January 1960.

Christopher Oyesiku in Amahl and the Night Visitor, 1965.

At a musical evening of selected men and women that lasted almost two hours in the residence of David Wehl, Principal Information Officer, British Deputy High Commissioner's office in Western Nigeria. The artistes were Janetta Mayer, accompanied on the piano by Irene Van Der Wall and Christopher Oyesiku, also accompanied by Ann Buchanan. Though the other two artists—Irene and Ann played their part well, I still think that I enjoyed (as did many others) Janetta and Christopher better. When Chris started to sing "Arm, Arm Ye Brave. . ." I told a colleague by my side, "what a dull song!" But as he continued I later fell in love with the song. This song was written in 1746 to celebrate the victory of William, Duke of Cumberland over Charles Edward, the Scottish Pretender. In it, Judas Maccabaeus is announced the future leader of the Israelites who eventually leads them to victory. Then came "We know No other Thought of Vengeance;" according to Chris, this interesting song is the second of the two great *arias* that are sung in the opera by Sarasto, the High Priest. The rendering of the song was done in a most perfect manner.

Another of Christopher Oyesiku's song was "Sea Fever" by John Ireland. Chris told me the words of what he called "this stirring song" are by the English Poet Laureate, John Masefield—"I must go down to the sea again; to the lonely sea and the sky. . ." A critic had this to say about the song: "This is a fine song in which both the words and the music are perfectly wedded together." One particular section of the program enjoyed most was the song in Yoruba written by Ayo Bankole. They were three—"Ja Itanna T'o Ntan," "Kiniun," and "Iya." The first one warns that "Never leave until tomorrow the good that can be done today;" the second tells about the power and influence of Lion (Kiniun), king of animals. It says when Lion roars in the forest, the entire forest become silent for fear of being killed by the king; and the third is called Mother, that explains how mothers care for their children and how helpful they are to them. This adaptation deserves commendation, and I think Chris should do more of it to justify the high respect the audience had for him during and after this show. Now I shall tell you something about Chris. While in England, he took part in both sacred and secular concerts and also in opera. He made many recitals on the BBC Overseas Service, and had the rare opportunity of appearing on BBC Television for the first time in 1960. Among the VIPs who watched the show were the Acting British Deputy High Commissioner, Roger Barltrop and the American Counsel in Western Nigeria, John Meagher.[9]

---

9   Bob Knockabout, "Musical Evening at David Wehl's—We Know No Thought of Vengeance," *Nigerian Tribune,* Tuesday, 29 May, 1962.

Christopher Oyesiku in a Song Recital.

The Goethe Institute had long sent out invitations to music lovers to converge at the Nigerian Institute for International Affairs to watch a concert performance by Christopher Oyesiku, Nigeria's well-known bass singer and musician, to be accompanied by a Bulgarian born pianist Emilia Jonakieva Hodgeva. And many music lovers including Ayo Bankole, was amongst the audience to see and hear other musicians perform. The hall was packed full. Oyesiku's rendering of the bass coupled with the effortless ease of Emilia Hodgeva's dexterity on the piano, raised applause and ovation from the audience. Somewhere in the middle of the night's performance, Oyesiku sang a medley of native Yoruba cultural repertoire. At the end of his singing, he told the audience: "Most of the Yoruba tunes you heard tonight are composed by the one and only musical virtuoso, Ayo Bankole, of the Department of Music, University of Lagos." At the mention of Ayo Bankole's name, all eyes looked at the back row where Bankole was sitting. He stood up with his ready smile on his lips, and moved towards the stage to be openly introduced to the audience by Christopher Oyesiku. As he ascended the stage, it was all cheers and ovation for the man who had composed such wonderful tunes. Other prominent person who stood near him in a mutual talk was the Director-General of the NBC, Christopher Kolade.

Christopher Oyesiku and Emilia Jonakieva Hodgeva at the
Nigerian Institute for International Affairs, Lagos, 1975.

**Christopher Oyesiku and Ayo Bankole at the
Italian Embassy, Lagos, 1975.**

The second part of the show started and we all got enveloped in the performance and carried away by the beautiful show, little suspecting that by the next morning, the man who composed some of the tunes would be a corpse. We did not leave the hall until 10:30 PM and we all happily left the premises of the Institute for International Affairs with sweet dreams of a greater tomorrow. On Saturday morning, the news of his death came to me like a nightmare. "It could not be." I tried to console myself. I tried to recollect his ready smile, his cute suit of the previous night. Bankole was in his musical elements then. He did not look like one going to die. The late Ayo Bankole is not just a fine musician, pianist and organist, but a renowned composer of tunes. His major accolade was his composition of the Second All-Africa Games anthem. He was busy preparing a new national anthem for the nation when tragedy struck at the most unholy hour of the morning. Little did Bankole realize that the last ovation he had at the International Institute was going to be his last and that his return gestures in appreciation of the cheering crowd was indeed his farewell smile. Though Bankole is dead, the musician in him will never die. His compositions will outlive and immortalize his name. As we mourn and sympathize with his bereaved daughter and relations, we should all learn to live with this threat of being clubbed to death in our own beds[10] and always remember that life is a passing thrill. It comes and goes. Today, it is the Bankoles, tomorrow, it could even be you. May their souls, rest in perfect peace.[11]

Bass Christopher Oyesiku marked his sixtieth anniversary recently with a piece of his art; he entertained guests with a song recital at the Nigerian Institute of International Affairs, Victoria Island, Lagos, in October, 1985. Oyesiku sings to the delight of a captivated audience. Among the notable dignitaries at the concert were John Okwesa, Dr.

---

10 Ayo Bankole and his wife Toro were both brutally murdered while sleeping by his own half brother in 1976.

11 Willy Bozimo, "Sad Exit of a Music Maestro," *Lagos Weekend,* Friday, 12 November, 1976.

Irene Thomas, and Sir Mobolaji Bank-Anthony. On the piano was Vincent Richter.[12]

Wednesday, 11 June, 1986, marks a new chapter in the music annals of the Italian Cultural Institute. On that day, a performing trio—Christopher Oyesiku, the Nigerian bass singer with four decades of experience behind him, with Vincent Richter, a Ghanaian pianist, and Jeanne Modder, a Sri Lankan pianist, will mount the stage for a night of classical music performances at the residence of the Italian Ambassador, 8 Eleke Crescent, Victoria Island, Lagos. The performance by the trio will cover the works of some late masters including Ayo Bankole, the Nigerian classical music legend, George Frederic Handel, J. B. Lully, and Wolfgang Amadeus Mozart. Other musicians whose works will be presented are M. De Falla and Frederic Chopin. This performance by the trio is a departure from the activities of the cultural institute that has made a mark as the most consistent in exhibiting Nigerian fine arts, while the center's musical performances are limited to visiting Italian performers. According to Gabriel le Tombini, director of the center, this is to show that the institute believes in the universality of art.[13]

There must surely be something classic about classical music that accounts for its resilience and drawing power till date. Through the centuries, through the revolutionary and technological changes in the shape of global pop music, classical music, though very much in the background has retained its solemnity, sometimes however, challenging one to ask what the whole thing is all about. Years ago, spanning about two and half centuries, classical music reigned supreme in Europe, treating nobles and the affluent to what was then considered nature's ultimate gifts—voices, compositions, and instrumental mastery. Then, Scarlatti, Vivaldi, Handel, Mozart, Bach and other such names achieved a glorious height, and Italian opera at the same time ruled the world of classical music. They worshipped the sopranos and reputed

---

12 *Lagos Life*, Thursday, 17 October, 1985.
13 Kafui Gale-Zoyiku, "A Night of the Classics," *The Guardian Supplement*, Sunday, 8 June, 1986.

conservatory-tested groups at this period in history; often performed in marbled arched monumental stages, declaring clear and definite the natural tunes as composed by the masters. The glory did not go without blemish; for youths and kids with signs of talent were then caught and castrated that they should remain forever providers of wonder and glory in the form of high vocal *tessitura;* that was then.

At an upper chamber of its embassy house last Wednesday, with every decorum and elegance, though not to the magnificence of the ancient Italian opera venues, the Italian Embassy hosted a concert of classical music, featuring Christopher Oyesiku—bass with Vincent Richter and Jeanne Modder on piano. With necks stretched, arms folded and legs crossed, the audience kept the silence as the performers took their turn; each earning applause as emolument at the end of performance. The air was cordial, the quietness total, and the end of performance applause regular and timely, but that did not eliminate the question I once asked Chief Ayo Rosiji: "what is the relationship with, meaning, and extent of understanding of Africans to this type of white collar music? And if classical music evolved as music for the bourgeois, must it remain so? If not, how come anytime classical music concert is held, the audience is made up of 'the lords,' the glaringly affluent?" Rosiji then explained lack of appreciation of classical music as dependent on exposure. He said: "If classical music is put into local idiom; more people will appreciate it." One cannot exactly tell how local the performance at the Italian Embassy was few days ago, but there was something clear from that night's performance—the talent and ability of Christopher Oyesiku at age sixty-one. Of course the bass soloist has established a mark for himself within the classical music circle in the country and even beyond, having tied himself to this form of music for the past twenty-six years. His performance at the Italian Embassy however reasserted his talent, and showed to his first time watchers, what the combination of talent, age, and maturity can produce in the area of artistic exhibition.

Beyond the monotonous and sometimes irritating sound of the classical piano, Oyesiku added life and humor to the music, even conscripting some parts of the audience to join his subtly. As the giggles and apparent excitement met his performance, the hypocrisy of all those stretched necks that handed out programmed claps to the end of every piano performance, became clear. Together with Oyesiku in this performance were Vincent Richter and Jeanne Modder, Ghanaian and Sri Lankan pianists respectively. Each ballyhooed well for his or her part, even though the imperious applause did not allow one to evaluate the actual appreciation of each artist's performance. Classical music might be a provider of high standard relaxation as Ayo Rosiji once said, but there is something that nudges the mind about this brand of music, telling one that not many Africans yet appreciate or understand what the music is all about. Amid the graveyard silence that accompanies a classical music performance and the expected applause that append the end of each rendition, there is a certain feeling that this music genre will for a long time to come remain a gentleman's music—no sweat, no effort, and no movement. Perhaps, there is something valuable to the human psyche from the absolute calmness that accompanies this form of music. Perhaps, still, people like Christopher Oyesiku puts life into it.[14]

It could have been described as quaint by the popular music circle. But it was saved this description because it was not designed for and made no pretention towards the popular music buffs. On Sunday, 7 July, 1991, a select audience in Lagos had the special privilege of experiencing a presentation of classical music at the Banquet Hall of L'Hotel Eko Meridien, courtesy of Ideas Communications and Benson and Hedges Music. It does not happen too often around here. Some cosmopolitans would say it doesn't happen enough. Although, efforts have been made by the likes of Pa Christopher Oyesiku, and organization like the Music Society of Nigeria, to impel classical music presentation to higher pedestal, those who have ears for it still appear to be at the odd end of the bargain. This fact makes the Sunday performance of

---

14   Andy Ezeani, "Oyesiku: The Classics Keep Their Class," *The Guardian*, Saturday, 14 June, 1986.

Joseph Haydn's oratorio, *The Creation,* an occasion to document and strengthen the hopes of Nigerian classical music *aficionados.* Featuring the Lagos-based City Chorale, led by Senator Lere Adesina and directed by Emeka Nwokedi. The concert starred three eminent Nigerian performers, Joy Nwosu Lo-Bamijoko (soprano), Lazarus Ekwueme (tenor), and Christopher Oyesiku (bass). They were the "Big Three." Briefly, and in line with the oratorical genre, the performance explored the Biblical story of Creation through a careful departmentalization, reconstruction and harmonization of various elements of oral delivery—the *recitatives,* the solos, the duets, the trios, and the choruses. In three parts, the performers enunciated the creation processes, setting the moods variously with the instrument and, progressively and evocatively translating oral traditions into a sort of ethereality. The creation of the firmament, of the waters, of the fields, and of lights in splendor bright, through the coming of man, flowed in the dexterous performance of Joy Nwosu as Angel Gabriel; Christopher Oyesiku as Raphael, with interpolated and re-enforcing entries by the chorus. Oyesiku's bass filled the hall only when it had to and it was a marvel to experience the aptitude of his vocal range from the highest possible pitch to the lowest decibel. For lovers of classical music, the Nwokedi-led performers seemed to have brought only a teacher. One could imagine, too, that the pianists, seasoned Richard Bucknor and Mrs. Tolu Obajimi, as well as the organist, Mr. Kayode Oni, would be itching for an epic dimension to their appearance last Sunday.[15]

---

15   Osibata, "City Chorale Joins the *Big Three* on Songs of Creation," *The Guardian,* Friday, 12 July, 1991.

**Christopher Oyesiku Singing at the Ayo Bankole's 70th
Anniversary Concert at the University of Cambridge, 2005.**

Christopher Oyesiku Singing at the Ayo Bankole's 70th Anniversary Concert at the University of Cambridge, 2005.

Anyone who saw the stars parade of FESTAC '77 choir and the celebrity showcase at the Trenchard Hall of the University of Ibadan, on Saturday, 7 October, 1995, will find it difficult to make a distinction. The actors were the same. Lazarus Ekwueme, Richard Bucknor, and Zeal Onyia, were core members of the famed FESTAC Choir and Dapo Adelugba, who directed *Langbodo,* Nigeria's drama entry for the same festival. The Saturday night event was to mark the seventieth birthday anniversary of the music *impresario,* Christopher Oyesiku, who himself directed the FESTAC Choir. Tagged *Celebrity Concert,* the event billed to start at 7:00 PM, began thirty minutes earlier because the hall was already jam packed. Tickets were already exhausted but people insisted they would stand. Such was the importance attached to the event and personality everybody on the University of Ibadan campus fondly called "Papa." On the dot of 7:00 PM, the man was ready to perform. Looking quite elegant in his cream colored double-breasted suit matched with a white shirt and lavender colored bow tie; Pa Oyesiku looked anything but seventy. As he walked up the aisle, the entire audience rose in reverence to the man who has greatly influenced the aggrandizement of classical music in Nigeria. In a spontaneous reaction, they all sang "Happy Birthday to You," and the man could only nod in acceptance of the best wishes showered on him.

It is time for Act One. On the bill is Pa Oyesiku himself and on the piano was Christopher Ayodele. In rendering Handel's *O Voi Del Mio Poter,* Xone's "The Star That Bids the Shepherd Fold," and Mozart's "Say Goodbye To Pastime and Play, Hard." He displayed the dexterity that verifies the claim that Pa Oyesiku remains the foremost bass singer in the country. He was irresistible and the appreciative audience was to give him another standing ovation. It definitely was his night and he did not fail them. His voice was a sheer delight. Lazarus Ekwueme who also sang at the concert, later told *The Guardian* that "Is She Not Passing Fair" was dedicated to the celebrant. "His singing, that is held in high esteem is comparable to the beauty of a fair lady that cannot go unnoticed," says Ekwueme. The University of Ibadan Choir directed by

Pa Oyesiku also thrilled the mammoth crowd with Handel's "Where'er You Walk," Thomas Keighley's "Come Let's Be Merry," and James Mansfield's "When My Lady Walks in Beauty." The renditions that were in the mood of the occasion, no doubt triggered more interests than some of the solo performances. It was also a testimony to the efforts of the *maestro* at the University of Ibadan. Largely peopled by students, the choir was excellent. At the end of the evening, the audience actually had a wonderful time, and Pa Oyesiku and the other star acts, did give people a value for their money while also stressing emphatically that he would be around for quite sometime to come. Later, Professor Adelugba told *The Guardian* that Papa Oyesiku has not only been a great asset to the Department of Theater Arts, but to the entire university. "As director of the UI Choir, he has set standards that will be difficult for amateur choirs to contend with. It is our hope that Papa will be allowed to continue the good work he has done so far, so that music will be put firmly on the map of our university life," says Adelugba.[16]

The Show tagged CELEBRITY CONCERT, was Christopher Oyesiku's idea of a seventieth birthday 'party.' "I express myself better in songs," Oyesiku announces to the audience in his appreciative monologue. "I have chosen concert to celebrate because of my life of music. . . Music puts a noble feeling in our lives. . . It is language by itself. . . I am always happiest when I am listening to music." Guest artists who joined Oyesiku to celebrate his "life of music" included, Prof. Dapo Adelugba, Ayo Bankole Jr., Zeal Onyia—whose performance with his trumpet with piano accompaniment, was so impressive that the audience was asking for an *encore*; Edward Boamah and Funmilayo Boamah, Prof. Mrs. Mosunmola Omibiyi Obidike, Richard Bucknor, and Lazarus Ekwueme. Christopher Oyesiku himself gave solo performances of a few numbers with his dainty bass voice, bearing a ring of authority roaring through the hall, while the audience that included the respected

---

16 Olayiwola Adeniji, "Melodies for the Master," *The Guardian*, Wednesday, 11 October, 1995.

historian, Prof. J. F. Ade Ajayi, dons, and foreigners, gave him a deserved ovation. The University of Ibadan Choir made up mostly of young undergraduates of the university, were also on hand to render good numbers in acknowledgment of a man who has taught them to sing good music, as the University of Ibadan Artist-In Residence for eight years. The renditions of the choir were so good that the audience thought they were students of the Music Department of the institution. The UI Choir was later to be described by Raymond Zard, the millionaire businessman, who was the chairman of the occasion, as, "the very best in the country."[17]

---

17 Wale Adebanwi, "Christopher Oyesiku at 70: Nigeria's Leading Musicologist and Virtuoso Clocks 70," *Sunday Tribune,* 15 October, 1995.

Chapter 4

Choral Concerts

Christopher Oyesiku graced Nigerian musical platforms in Lagos, Ibadan, Ilesha, and Nsukka, with some of the most beautiful choral songs ever performed in that country. These songs were written by famous composers from all around the world—African, American, Latin-American, Caribbean, European, and Nigerian. From a period that spanned from 1963 to 1997, Oyesiku single-handedly directed four magnificent choirs: the Lagos Musical Society Choir, the Nigerian Broadcasting Corporation Choir—Radio Nigeria, the Oyo State College of Education Choir, Ilesha, and the University of Ibadan Choir. He trained these choirs to perform at a very enviable lofty standard that always leaves their audiences screaming for *encore* at the end of every concert. Their performances were always eclectic, electrifying, emotive, joyful, impeccable, crisp, energetic, flawless, and intercultural. The intonation, diction, phrasing, enunciation, balance and attack were always with precision and accuracy. One may then ask at this juncture, how did Oyesiku pulled-off this extraordinary feat in a nation where art music belongs to an exiguous moiety of the populace? How did he arouse the interests of his Nigerian choirs to sing global intercultural songs in multiple tongues? How did he train and motivate his choirs to sing European classical music? How did he wow his audiences? And what are the secrets behind his consistent successes in choral concerts?

Christopher Oyesiku the Conductor.

Choral Training

Out of the four choirs he directed, Oyesiku inaugurated the University of Ibadan Choir and that of the Oyo State College of Education, Ilesha. In his approach to the training and working with all these choirs, he adhered strictly to what he regarded as the 'essentials of voice production' and these include:

1. Breathing and vocal techniques—the throat is the temple of the voice.
2. Exercises at every choir practice to gain vocal quality and strength.
3. The establishment of choral unity and blending of the voices.
4. Good diction.
5. Interpretation of the music, and
6. The establishment of firm discipline, whilst maintaining a cordial relationship with the choir.

Lagos Musical Society Choir

Practices and performances with the Lagos Musical Society Choir from 1963 to 1970 were enjoyable, because there was less difficulty in making the singers understood instructions. The choir was composed of both European and Nigerians who had reasonable musical knowledge, and were thus able to learn pieces without too much drudgery. As the years passed, both the Europeans and Nigerians with practical singing skills reduced in numbers, and more time had to be spent on teaching vocal techniques to each part separately. Less time was spent on learning the music. In spite of Oyesiku's efforts to recruit new members, the size of the choir dwindled, and practice venues became difficult to find; thus, he had to disband the choir in 1981.

**Christopher Oyesiku Conducting the
Lagos Musical Society Choir, 1968.**

Lagos Musical Society Choir in Christmas Carol Concert at the Cathedral Church of Christ, Lagos, in the Presence of Brigadier and Mrs. Mobolaji Johnson, 1971.

Nigerian Broadcasting Corporation Choir

In recruiting for the NBC Choir, Oyesiku had to audition and admit sopranos with no musical knowledge. Oyesiku based his selection on those with good education and a flair for music, as well as those who were willing to work hard. The men were better positioned as most of them came from church choirs and had some musical experience, though they lacked vocal training. They had three rehearsals a week with emphasis on training for the ladies at one of them, since most of the ladies had no musical knowledge. Apart from training the voices, Oyesiku had to drum the music into them. Hard work paid-off, and in spite of various setbacks, he achieved an excellent standard and was able to perform sacred and secular choral works, including the music of the Cathedral Church of Christ, Lagos, such as anthems, responses, chanting of the Psalms and special settings of canticles. During those years, the choir broadcast an evening service every Sunday. The choir was also in demand for special services and other state occasions. It formed the core of the choir that recorded the current National Anthem of Nigeria. It also served as a beacon for other choirs by setting an exemplary standard. This outstanding achievement was only possible through the hard work and dedication of choir members. Similar to the Lagos Musical Society Choir, Oyesiku directed the NBC Choir from 1963 to 1981.

Christopher Oyesiku Conducting the NBC Choir at the Cathedral Church of Christ, Lagos, 1974.

Oyo State College of Education Choir

In 1982, Oyesiku accepted an invitation to chair the Department of Music at the Oyo State College of Education, Ilesha. However, on his arrival, Oyesiku was very disappointed by the complete lack of musical knowledge of the students admitted from Grade II teacher training colleges, who claimed to have met the entry requirements. Oyesiku quickly realized that three years would not be sufficient to equip the students even with the basic music knowledge. He then made an unprecedented move to petition the college authorities for a need to extend the curriculum by an extra year. The approval of his proposition changed the training of the students from three years to a four-year program. Prior to his arrival, most of the students were unable to sing the tonic solfa and did not know what a stave looked like. Students with the basic Grade II paper qualifications were therefore admitted through auditions and interviews. Teaching these students was a very daunting task. Fortunately, the college had adequate facilities for the Department of Music. There were practice rooms with pianos and rooms large enough for class teaching and choir training. Oyesiku and the other music lecturers worked very hard to teach these students to the standard that substantiates their competency in music teaching. He formed the school's choir and taught singing, history, and rudiments of music.

Oyesiku worked with the students from morning to late in the evening, and the students often practiced at night. As would be expected, it was immensely strenuous, but was rewarded by the fact that the students responded with enthusiasm and appreciated the efforts of the music faculty. All the students studied singing—a principal study in school music, and had to join the choir where they learnt the essentials of voice production, speech and acting, as well as repertoires for class teaching. Oyesiku encouraged the students to enroll for the external examinations of the Associated Board of the Royal Schools of Music, London. They performed well enough in the first year for the ABRSM examiner from London to come to Ilesha, and examined the students in voice and piano at the college. In the second year of training, the choir performed its first concert. It was well received and the concert became a quarterly event. The group was so popular that it was invited to perform Christmas carol concerts at the Anglican and Methodist Cathedrals in Ilesha.

University of Ibadan Choir

In January 1986, Oyesiku received an invitation from Professor Ayo Banjo, the Vice-Chancellor of the University of Ibadan. The purpose was to help to resuscitate the musical life of the academic community and to raise a choir for the university. Oyesiku accepted the position of Artist-In-Residence on 1 March, 1987. He regarded this appointment as a great opportunity to restore the musical life of the university and encourage the appreciation of art music; to develop a university choir of international standard, and to cultivate musical interaction between town and gown.[18] During his ten years at the university, Oyesiku was able, without the assistance of any other music faculty or any music vote, to achieve most of his objectives with huge successes. It was an uphill task as there was no music department at the institution. He was attached to the Department of Theater Arts, where there were no music courses. Oyesiku was back to square one again; that is, building the music foundation from the scratch—ground zero. He had to recruit singers from any department of the university who were willing to join the choir. To further complicate the process, he had to teach each part of the songs separately as most of the singers could not read music nor had any vocal training.

---

18 Town and gown is a Nigerian phrase denoting the regular people or citizens in the surrounding community of a college or university (town) and the academic coterie on the actual university campus (gown). Hence, town and gown: public and campus.

**Christopher Oyesiku Conducting at the Trenchard Hall,
University of Ibadan.**

Oyesiku successfully raised a choir of sixty voices, and with dogged determination and hard work, coupled with persuasion; he was able to keep the choir going until he retired in 1997. This was in spite of the yearly turnover and incessant strikes by administrative staff, faculty, and students. The choir members often stayed for little more than one semester in the group; it was not until his last couple of years that he had up to thirty percent of the members that had taken part in the previous concerts. Another disincentive was the fact that the choir members could not receive any credits for their participation in the group, even though they spent six hours a week at rehearsals. Also, because music was not widely appreciated on the university campus, their student colleagues made fun of them. On a positive note, by the time Oyesiku retired, the choir had become very popular and recruitment was easier. He worked the choir tirelessly on breathing exercises, vowels shaping, breathing, resonance, and flexibility. The songs were learned by rote; each part separately and then together. As Oyesiku had several years of experience in teaching voice production, he was successful in obtaining good quality singing from his fourth choir. The university choir was in great demand; in fact, it performed at the wedding of the daughter of Chief Emeka Anyaoku, former Secretary General of the Commonwealth. The choir's first major concert was for the fortieth anniversary of the University of Ibadan, in November 1988, where the university anthem was premiered. The anthem became a regular feature at convocation (commencement) ceremonies and at other performances.

During Oyesiku's tenure as Artist-In-Residence, the choir participated in fifty-one concerts: thirty-six for the university and fifteen for the Music Circle of the university, of which Oyesiku became the President during his first year at the institution. Oyesiku expressed his gratitude to the lovers of classical music in Ibadan, who generously donated funds to organize the concerts. He thoroughly enjoyed his years at Ibadan. His only regret was that he could not persuade the university administration to develop a music department. Oyesiku remained grateful and indebted to Professor Ayo Banjo, for giving him the wonderful opportunity to contribute his musical skill and knowledge to the great premier University in Nigeria.

Choral Reviews

Following are some selected newspaper reviews of choral concerts directed by *maestro* Christopher Oyesiku in Lagos and Ibadan, from 1971 to 1992:

It was Carol singing day at Dodan Barracks, residence of General Yakubu Gowon, yesterday. The Nigerian Broadcasting Corporation Choir, conducted by Christopher Oyesiku, NBC head of music, sang Christmas Carols for the Head of State and Mrs. Gowon, as well as some invited guests. General Gowon charms the choristers with his ready humor after the carol singing.[19]

---

19 *Daily Times,* "Carol Singing at Dodan Barracks," Friday, 31 December, 1971.

**Christopher Oyesiku with General Yakubu Gowon and
First Lady Victoria Gowon and the NBC Choir, at the
Dodan Barracks, Lagos, 1971.**

It was a parade of stars. An evening of classical music embellished with a few popular yet ever suitable folk songs. The songs were rendered by the different groups and artistes that included the University of Ibadan Choir, Christopher Oyesiku, Femi Akinkugbe, Joy Nwosu Lo-Bamijoko, Joyce Lowe, Michael Hudson, Om'te Diachavbe, and Amorelle Inanga. It turned out to be a long list of tunes from masters of the opera and classical music, both at home and abroad. Great tunes from men like the legendary composer and director, Mozart, Schubert, Chopin, Norman Stone, Sullivan, Ayo Bankole, Dayo Dedeke and Ekundayo Phillips, featured prominently and left their impact on the audience. The occasion was the fortieth Anniversary Celebration Concert of the University of Ibadan, on Saturday, 12 November, 1988. It was organized by the Department of Theater Arts of the university. The concert was sponsored by Elf Nigeria Limited.

At the center of the show was the University of Ibadan Choir that came up on three inspiring occasions to delight the moderate crowd. In between their appearances came the other singers and pianists. Formed early last year, the choir, made up of thirty-three ladies and seventeen gentle men, set the songs tumbling down twenty-five minutes behind schedule. Gracefully they sang the university anthem with a lot of pride that sent the audience cheering and glad for the encomiums rained on the beloved premier university. The choir did not disappoint the university's Vice-Chancellor, Professor Ayo Banjo, his wife Alice, and Mr. and Mrs. Michael Romieu, the Chief Executive of Elf Nigeria Limited. The choir followed this up with Henry Purcell's piece, "In These Delightful, Pleasant Groves." The song reaffirmed the joyous mood of the university. With Christopher Oyesiku bringing his wealth of experience to bear on the group as its conductor and director, they sang other reputable tunes that included "Sweet and Lot," "Come Let's Be Merry," "The Blue Danube," "Courage and Trust," and "The Blessedness of Work." The choir's accompanist, Emmanuel Boamah, a Cape Coast University music graduate, was electrifying on the piano, so was the rhythmic beats of Chris Oyesiku's brilliant conducting.[20]

Tonight, 7 May, 1989, at 7:30 PM, the advertized concert of choral and instrumental music began in the presence of the Vice-Chancellor, Ayo Banjo, and his soft-spoken music loving wife, Mrs. Alice Banjo. The guests of honor, Chief, Dr. and Mrs. Olu I. Akinkugbe, sat to the right hand of Professor and Mrs. Banjo in the front row of the auditorium. Virtually all the seats, both on the lower and upper levels, had been occupied by an audience now accustomed to the delights of the Christopher Oyesiku directed concerts of the Department of Theater Arts, and concern to begin on time. In spite of this, there were over fifty persons waiting to purchase their tickets at the central Porter's Lodge at curtain time. These late-comers had to content themselves with the spare seats in the aisles, and, when these had been occupied, the rest, stood behind the back rows of the upper and lower levels in the hall. The music concerts at the University of Ibadan may well force the hands of the authorities into providing on campus an auditorium of the magnitude of the National Theater Main Bowl or, at least, of the dimensions and aesthetic beauty of the Oyo State Cultural Center Main Auditorium, on Mokola Hill, Ibadan. The University of Ibadan Choir and the entire audience stood up, at the behest of Christopher Oyesiku. The choir sang the university anthem, the words of which had been written by Isidore Ekpewho, a Professor of English at the University of Ibadan, and whose music had been created by the veteran composer and organist, Olaolu Omideyi. Omideyi was an erstwhile Lecturer in music at the University of Ibadan, Faculty of Education, who now runs his own school of music. For those who saw the beginnings of the University of Ibadan Choir barely two years ago, and the long hours of patient work Christopher Oyesiku had put in to turn a relatively amateur set of volunteers—house wives, university lecturers from various disciplines,

---

20   Babatunde Ajayi, "U.I. Concert: A Night to Remember," *The Guardian,* Tuesday, 6 December, 1988.

university students with varying degrees of initial commitment and, mercifully, a handful of professionals—into a coherent and fascinating team; the rendering of the university anthem by the survivors of that early group (and it takes zeal and commitment to survive the rigors of Christopher Oyesiku's training and rehearsal sessions) must have come as a very delight.

The Vice-Chancellor and all the principal officers, the staff, and the alumni of the university in the auditorium, must have contributed their fair share to the very warm rounds of applause that very quickly, became the regular feature of the evening—so engaging was every item in the package, as we were to see and hear. When Amorelle Inanga mounted the dais, followed a few steps behind by Christopher Oyesiku, a new round of applause began. The audience knew that the first half of the evening was to be brought to a close by the Inanga-Oyesiku pair. Amorelle Inanga was confident and sure-finger in her piano accompaniment of the four pieces the *maestro* sang, and this time, Christopher Oyesiku's choices did greater justice to his immense talent than the choices for the 30 March, 1989 concert. Handel, Lully, Arne, and Mozart were honored with Christopher Oyesiku's rendition of their songs: Handel's *Si Tra I Ceppi,* Lully's *Bois Epais* (Sombre Woods), Arne's "Now Phoebus Sinketh in the West," and from Mozart's *The Marriage of Figaro,* Christopher Oyesiku chose a fitting final *aria* for this four-piece performance, "Say Goodbye Now to Pastime and Play, Lad."

The ten minute interval was followed by an unusual rounds of ovation that tonight were louder and longer than in the music concerts we had witnessed in the past two years at Trenchard Hall. Christopher Oyesiku has become a very rare darling of Trenchard Hall audiences. There is good reason to believe that Uncle Christopher Oyesiku will see the University of Ibadan to the pinnacle of national glory in music in the years immediately ahead. The choir was at its best in the final piece, "To the Inn Where Bagpipes Sound." The *encore* on account of the very loud and long ovation of the audience led to a standing ovation by the entire audience. J. S. Bach must have turned in his grave tonight, and Christopher Oyesiku and his team of artists went home with contentment after the final bow and congratulatory hand shakes by Professor and Mrs. Banjo. Trenchard Hall is now undoubtedly a cultural center for music. The University of Ibadan, Department of Theater Arts, that aspires to developing her programs in drama, music, dance, design, visual arts, media arts (radio, television, film, folk media), speech/rhetorical arts, and arts management, more fully than it has been able to do so far, does perhaps have a promising basis for the further development of the music wing of its curriculum in the Oyesiku Music concerts.[21]

The opening scene at each performance is usually colorful. At the well-lit famous Trenchard Hall of the University of Ibadan, the choir enters the stage in two uniform lines. The women were dressed in sparkling white blouse and long black skirts, while the men attired in well-starched white long sleeve shirts matched with black bow tie, black pair of trousers, and black shoes. Like an experienced professional who has an enviable mastery over his trade, Christopher O. Oyesiku in immaculate white shirt, white coat, laced with a black bow tie, and a black pair of shoes, shining under his black pair of trousers, walked into the hall with an infectious confidence. The group bowed slightly as a sign of courtesy, and the audience responded by cheering and clapping their hands. As these acceptable rituals were taking place, Emmanuel Boamah, an experienced pianist, walked diligently to the stage and took his seat with his eyes fixed to the musical notes and his hands ready to push down on the appropriate keys on the piano. As usual, and as a sign of gratitude, the tune, university anthem was the first song performed by the choir. Backing the audience, and holding the slender baton on his right hand, he looked straight at both his group and the pianist and raised his two hands slightly above his head. The green light was thus given, and the choir began the evening's performance.

---

21   Dapo Adelugba, "Memorable Musical Night at Trenchard Hall," *Daily Sketch,*
      Wednesday, 5 July, 1989.

During the late 1950s and early 1960s, the University of Ibadan, apart from being a center of knowledge, had the added reputation of encouraging musical concerts. That was a period when there existed a large community of Europeans residing there as university faculty and administrators in both public and private sectors of the Nigerian economy. Moreover, anywhere there are dramatic arts music becomes an indispensable company. Ibadan being known also as bubbling city of both English and African drama, witnessed the active presence of Yoruba and English musical concerts. From the mid-sixties, there was a gradual shift of preference for English musical concerts to purely indigenous African music. This was due to the massive exodus of Europeans and an insipient spirit of nationalism and patriotism. However, as music generally enriches itself through national and foreign sourcing, the gradual recrudescence of European musical concerts at the University of Ibadan is not altogether surprising. This resurgence has also creatively integrated African music and tunes. The author of this musical resuscitation is Christopher Oyesiku—Nigerian veteran soloist and pragmatic musicologist. "This on-going effort at reintroducing and re-injecting musical concerts into the life of our community and also for the benefit of lovers of music in general, could not have been achieved without the encouragement and support of Professor Ayo Banjo—the Vice-Chancellor of the university," declared Oyesiku, who is an Artist-In-Residence at the University's Theater Arts Department. This year alone, the University of Ibadan Concert Group has had two successful performances that took place in April and September. "We shall also entertain the public on 13 November of this year during the university's convocation ceremony (commencement)," Oyesiku revealed. The April performance was initiated in order to raise funds for the restoration of Queen Elizabeth female hostel that was gutted by fire. The performance by Oyesiku's choir reportedly spurred the audience to donating a highly substantial amount of money towards the rapid restoration of the damaged hostel.

The concert choir consists of about fifty members including eighteen sopranos, twelve tenors, eleven altos, and nine basses. Its membership is drawn from students, graduates, doctors, engineers, teachers, and retired civil servants. After several hours of coaching and training, three days each week, Oyesiku has largely succeeded in blending and molding them into a group of highly talented individuals with diverse musical backgrounds. The classical music of George Frederic Handel (1685-1759) is another work usually given a preferential choice in the repertoire of songs rendered by Oyesiku's choir. Famous among these selected songs of Handel are "Let Their Celestial Concerts All Unite," "Where're You Walk" *(Semele)* as arranged for SATB by Thomas Keighley, and the "Arrival of the Queen of Sheba" as arranged for SATB by Weissmann. No doubt, the deafening ovation by the experienced audience that saluted the performance of these songs was a testimony to the level of musical expertise demonstrated by the choir. They later curtsy before the appreciative audience and moved out in the same disciplined manner they had entered the stage. The closing night was a watershed of mostly Nigerian songs. Compositions such as "My Way's Cloudy" by Fela Sowande, "Ojo Maaro" ("Rainfall") by Ayo Bankole, "E Jeun T'o Dara" ("Eat Healthy Food") and "Iwe Kiko" ("Education") both by Dayo Dedeke—all Nigerian songs, were part of the closing melodious songs. The very last song in the September performance was however, Thomas Dunhill's "Tubal Cain." Oyesiku explained the form and content of this song in the following terms: "This ballad tells of Tubal Cain who was a smith in days gone by." The tremendous success of this musical concert group, within a relatively short span of its renewed existence, is ascribed to the tireless efforts of Christopher Oyesiku.[22]

Unlike the last outing of the Unibadan Choir that was slightly marred by poor lighting of the hall, this time around, Trenchard Hall was well lit and the stage neatly covered with sparkling green rugs (carpets). This occasion coincided with the forty-second anniversary celebration of the University of Ibadan. Amongst those who were

---

22 "The Return of Classical Music," *The Guardian,* 7 October, 1990.

present in the hall full to capacity, and who gave both social and material support, were Professor Ayo Banjo, the Vice-Chancellor, his wife Mrs. Banjo, Mrs. Kola Daisi, apologizing for the absence of her husband, and Raymond Zard and his wife. It was the University of Ibadan Choir, made up of twenty-eight ladies and twenty men who raised the classical curtain with melodious rendition of the university anthem in which the virtues of sound knowledge and hard work were extolled. With Christopher Oyesiku as conductor and Emmanuel Boamah as accompanist, this experienced choir sang "Come Let's Be Merry," "Since First I Saw Your Face," "The Lass with a Delicate Air," and "A Choral Suite" of three verses composed by Thomas Ekundayo Phillips. The third verse of the suite carried inspiring words from Abraham Lincoln: "With malice towards none with charity for all, with firmness in the right, let us strive to finish the work we have begun." The audience responded with enthused ovation. One could perceive an inner joy transferred like electric current unto the beaming face of Christopher Oyesiku who was gladdened by the response of the audience. The concluding part of the concert heightened the inexhaustible talents of Christopher Oyesiku. Accompanied by Professor Sven Hansell, Oyesiku with his naturally talented bass voice sang *recit: O Voi Del Mio Poter, aria: Sorge Infausta Una Procella (Orlando)*—all by Handel, and "Verrat" by Brahms. The song, "Ja Itanna T'o Ntan," a music composed by Ayo Bankole, again, sang by Oyesiku, thrilled the audience.

The well-groomed University of Ibadan Choir closed the evening with four songs, last of which was a popular Yoruba folkloric tune, titled, "Iwe Kiko." A song of four verses "that tries to show that academic knowledge by itself is not sufficient equipment for life." The first verse stressed the importance of farming. The second verse expresses the love of the Yoruba for pounded yam or *gari* eaten with melon seed vegetable soup—product of the farm. In the third verse, the necessity for wisdom and understanding is explained. At the end of the song, a deafening ovation greeted the choir as they trouped out of the stage with confidence, showing signs of well grooming through the skillful supervision of Christopher and Femi Oyesiku.[23]

Christopher Oyesiku, Director of the University of Ibadan Choir and President of the Music Circle, once again, gave Trenchard Hall the aura of his now very well known and laudable music concerts on Sunday, 29 March, 1992. The most remarkable aspect of the evening's concert was the large number of new items in the group's repertory and the addition of one very highly gifted and inspired virtuoso-soprano, Etta Onyuike-Azih, to Christopher Oyesiku's team of guest artists. The concert began with the well rehearsed entry procession of members of the University Choir in their resplendent white-and-black evening outfits, white long-sleeved blouses and shirts with black bow ties, black long dresses and trousers with immaculate black shoes to match. Surrounded by Elaine Jegede's discreetly chosen and well arranged flowers on the stairs, on the dais and in the background; the choir in four rows, arranged in a concave manner to simulate a musical instrument, looked absolutely right for the occasion of ushering in Professor A. B. O. O. Oyediran into his new role as Nigeria's premier University's Vice-Chancellor. A role in which the choir and the fully packed rows of audience on the ground floor, and in the gallery of Trenchard Hall, clearly wished Professor Oyediran success and joy. The university anthem was followed by Norman Stone's "Come, Let's Be Merry," John Farmer's "To Take the Air," Johann Strauss Jr.'s *Wein, Weib and Gessing* op. 333, arranged for SATB by Henry Geehi. Finally, in this section of the evening's concert, the choir rendered "God's Gonna Buil' Up Zion's Wall," as arranged by Jester Hairston.

---

23   Tunde Fatunde, "Unibadan Choir, in Blissful Blasts of Sound and Voices, Lights Up Trenchard Hall," *The Guardian*, Saturday, 8 December, 1990.

**Christopher Oyesiku Conducting the
University of Ibadan Choir, 1992.**

Christopher Oyesiku, for all the numbers, was in top form as conductor and Adeniran Obasa played the piano quite well. The University of Ibadan Choir left no doubt in anyone's mind that they had taken several more steps towards total accomplishment since their last concert and that they had broadened their repertory of songs. After the donation had been received, the next section of the evening concert was the performance of the bass singer, Christopher Oyesiku, to the exquisite piano accompaniment of the brilliant Amorelle Inanga. Amorelle Inanga and Christopher Oyesiku, with the three pieces they rendered, proved their mettle to the Trenchard Hall audience. The pieces were Handel's *recit,* "I Feel the Deity Within," and *aria,* "Arm, Arm Ye Brave (*Judas Maccabeus*), Verdi's *aria – O Tu Palermo, Terra Adorata (I Vespri Siciliani),* and finally, Ayo Bankole's "Ja Itanna T'o Ntan." The re-entry of the splendidly attired ladies and gentlemen of the University Choir and the concave arrangement on the steps leading up to the stage of Trenchard Hall, marked the beginning of the end of an evening of choice music. The emphasis in the final section on modern Nigerian neo-classical composers' works was apt.

Apart from the opening piece to Adeniran Obasa's skillful piano accompaniment, "Just As The Tide, Was Flowing," arranged by Vaughan Williams, the remaining four pieces were Nigerian compositions, all charmingly conducted, accompanied and sung: Fela Sowande's "Steal Away," Dayo Dedeke's "E Jeun T'o Dara," Ayo Bankole's "Orisa Bi Ofun Kosi" ("There is None, Like the god of Throat"), and finally, the conductor's special, favorite, "Ojo Maaro" by Ayo Bankole. The Deputy Vice-Chancellor, Professor Olusola Akinyele, was a most charming host and the Vice-Chancellor, Professor Kayode Oyediran, when invited to make an address, praised the efforts of his predecessor, Professor Ayo Banjo, in encouraging the growth of music and thanked Christopher Oyesiku for revitalizing the musical life of the university. The Vice-Chancellor promised to entrench the creative arts at Ibadan in a significant and long lasting manner during his tenure of office.[24]

Christopher Oyesiku, with his accustomed repertory of regulars, the University of Ibadan Choir, and guest artistes, all of whom are now very well known to Trenchard Hall audiences, presented on Friday, 24 July, 1992, a most stirring and thoroughly refreshing End-of-Session Concert. What is remarkable about the July concert was the newness of most of the pieces rendered by the choir and the deliberate departure by all the guest artists from the pieces with which they had come to be identified by Trenchard Hall audience. The key-phrase for the evening's outfit was, undoubtedly, renewal and renovation. It was as if, in his sixth end-of-session concert since taking up his current appointment as the Artist-In-Residence at the University of Ibadan, Pa Oyesiku was challenging his audience in the colloquial Americanism, "You ain't seen nothing yet!" For, as conductor, he attacked each piece rendered by his choir with a new agility and a sense of enjoyment with every limb and muscle of his anterior and posterior physicality, for his singers and his audience. The rousing rendition of the university anthem with appropriate modulation, inflection and range, raised a patriotic applause from the Ibadan undergraduates, staff, and alum, and no less enthusiastic acclamation from other members on the 24 July audience. The tone-setter for the evening was followed by the choir's rendition of Michael Arno's "The Lass with Delicate Air" arranged for SATB by John West. William Paxton's "Breathe Soft, Ye Wonds," was no less beautifully rendered. William Rains "When My Lady Walks Beautifully," marked the end of the choir's first singing.

The second part of the evening's fare began with Christopher Oyesiku's renditions as bass and Amorelle Inanga charming, as usual, on the piano. They rendered four pieces—Thomas Arne's *recit*, "The Star that Bids the Shepherd Fold" and his *aria*, "Now Phoebus Sinketh in

---

24 Dapo Adelugba, "A Concert With A Difference," *Daily Sketch*, Saturday, 18 April, 1992.

the West," Johannes Brahms's "Verrat," and John Hatton's "Simon the Cellarer." Significantly, the neo-classical Nigerian composers' pieces, a few of which are the director's special favorites, were omitted from the 24 July concert. This must have been intentional. The director probably wants his audience to come to terms with the universality of the appeal of classical music, with or without Nigerian variants and derivatives. If this guess is correct, it must be added, then, that the point has been successfully made. Also, if Ibadan is pulling its weight in music, the area of drama and dance, in which the University of Ibadan had established reputation are being carefully watched for the new goods they have to deliver. Hard-earned reputations can only be sustained, or in some pitiful cases, resurrected, through diligent and painstaking effort. Therefore, Hats-off to Christopher Oyesiku, for re-kindling Ibadan's artistic flame.[25]

---

25 Dapo Adelugba, "UI Reviews Its End of Session Concert," *Daily Sketch*, Thursday, 20 August, 1992.

Christopher Oyesiku and the University of Ibadan Choir, 1995.

Christopher Oyesiku and the University of Ibadan Choir, 1997.

Recently, Rotary International District 9130 of Nigeria, in collaboration with the University of Ibadan Music Circle, presented 'A Musical Evening' at Trenchard Hall, University of Ibadan. It was another music concert in the accustomed delightful style of Christopher Oyesiku, with the difference that the Rotary auspices gave from time to time a new aspect to the evening. It was a merry evening. One suspects that the merry cheers of some members of the audience might have been induced by the tedium of long conference hours before the concert and a few pre-concert Sherries. Some of the Rotary International officers seemed to have taken the co-hosting of the concert somewhat, literally by mounting the stage and turning the pianist's fan off as he gently drew attention, in a mime performance, to the tenderness of the music sheets. The competition between the sound of music and that of polite chit-chat, occasionally became somewhat stiff—an unusual event at the Trenchard Hall concerts and an odd twist to the word 'musical' in the title of the evening's fare. In spite of these surprises, the evening's outfit was splendid. The University of Ibadan Choir conducted by Christopher Oyesiku, drew attention to the often forgotten beauty of the National Anthem and followed this with four elegant pieces--"Where're You Walk" (*Semele*) arranged for SATB by Thomas Reighley, "My Bonnie Lass" by John Brydson, "Far Away" arranged for SATB by Arthur Pearson, and "God's Gonna Buil' Up Zion's Wall" by Jester Hairston. The increasing variety in the repertory of the University of Ibadan Choir and the director's determination to uphold good performance standards deserve praise.

Christopher Oyesiku as bass and Amorelle Inanga as pianist, came on stage and the audience knew that they were in for another splendid treat before the intermission. Ponchielli's *Scena ed aria, La Turbini e Farnetichi (La Giocanda)*, and Wolfe's "Short'ning Bread," were a thrill. The University of Ibadan Choir filed in once again through the auditorium central aisle and, with the grand entry of the conductor, Christopher Oyesiku, whose bow was as usual, acknowledged with warm applause. The final section of the evening's show began after the conductor's signal to the pianist. Brahms' "Love, Fare Thee Well," followed by three memorable pieces by Nigerian neo-classical composers—Ayo Bankole's "Orisa Bi Ofun Kosi," Dayo Dedeke's "E je Ki a Sise O" ("Let Us Work"), and finally, Christopher Oyesiku's special, Ayo Bankole's "Ojo Maa Ro," that was *encored* by the merry audience, especially the Rotarians.

Christopher Oyesiku has often been praised for his virtuosity as bass singer, his adroitness as a conductor and his ingenuity in training and directing the University of Ibadan Choir. Attention should also be drawn to his managerial sagacity, drive, and innovativeness. These qualities have made it possible for musical concerts to become regular and to attain a new vigor in the last five years at Ibadan, and it is fair to believe that, as the Vice-Chancellor, Professor A. B. O. O. Oyediran has recently indicated, we are at the threshold of a period of resurgence for the creative arts. Christopher Oyesiku's tenacity of purpose sets a pattern that up-and-coming men and women of the arts can emulate.[26]

---

26 Dapo Adelugba, "A Musical Evening," *Daily Sketch,* Thursday, 15 October, 1992.

Chapter 5

Encomiums

Christopher Oyesiku has been praised and honored by several personalities, diplomatic corps, institutions and organizations in Nigeria and around the world for his extraordinary contributions to the development of classical music in Nigeria. These encomiums served as zest and booster to his imaginative mind and his acumen in art music in general. The following is representative of the numerous accolades and eulogies bestowed on Oyesiku:

Akintola Williams, after a service of Nine Lessons and Carols writes: "It is such a long time since I last heard so beautiful rendition of the piece from Handel's *Messiah* as it was rendered by your choir on Monday, 24 December, 1979."

The Honorable Kayode Esho after the NBC Choir had sung at the wedding service of his daughter, in a letter written on 6 January, 1981, admits: "This is to thank you for the most wonderful performance you and your choir put up in Ilesha at the wedding of my daughter. It is the consensus of opinion in Ilesha that there had been nothing like it since the inception of Christianity in that town."

The late Chief E. O. Okunowo following the NBC Choir's performance at the wedding of his daughter, in a letter dated 25 April,

1981, remarks: "I cannot adequately express how joyful I was, other than to say that I was wonderfully impressed by your excellent performance, and I wish to assure you that the memory of the occasion will be an indelible one in me and that generations yet unborn will learn of it from my record."

Daily Sketch, 20 December, 1987, after a concert held at Saint Peter's Anglican Church, Aremo, Ibadan, recounts: "*The Messiah* followed and Christopher Oyesiku's voice was a sheer delight. This was followed by Purcell's *An Evening Hymn* sung by Christopher Oyesiku, standing at the head of the aisle, his voice filling the entire church building with its booming splendor."

Professor Ayo Banjo in a letter written on 7 May, 1990, drops this line: "May I also take this opportunity again, to express my personal appreciation and that of the entire university, for your outstanding contributions to the cultural life of the university in the last few years."

Professor A. B. O. O. Oyediran in a letter dated 18 November, 1994, after the forty-sixth Foundation Day Ceremonies, showers words of gratitude: "On behalf of the entire University of Ibadan community, I wish to thank you for your excellent contributions to the success of our forty-sixth Foundation Day Celebrations. We appreciate the Musical Concert held on 14 November 1994 . . . We also thank you for the solo performance that added color to the proceedings on Thursday, 17 November, 1994."

Christopher Oyesiku.

Christopher Oyesiku and the University of Ibadan Choir, 1995.

In an article titled, "Tribute to a Virtuoso," Professor Dapo Adelugba of the Faculty of Arts, University of Ibadan, writes:

It gives one great joy to see the growth of an audience for music concerts at the University of Ibadan since the arrival on the staff of the Department of Theater Arts, of veteran singer and choir trainer, Christopher Oyesiku, who has only just begun his third year as Artist-in-Residence. The University of Ibadan has been treated to a steady diet of music concerts and of evening of performance by the University Choir, that Oyesiku has built from amongst professionals, amateurs, and students' singers in Ibadan. Among the highlights of the university choir's achievements is the impressive rendition of the new University of Ibadan anthem whose words were written by Professor Isidore Okpewho of the Department of English of the university and whose music was composed by veteran composer and organist, Olaolu Omideyi, who had been on the staff of the Faculty of Education of the university as lecturer in music in recent years. The tact, warmth, and aesthetic tastes of Uncle Christopher Oyesiku have made it possible for him to treat the Ibadan community to evenings of concerts by guest pianists, guest singers, guest librettists, and guest composers. These musicians come from as far away as Lagos and Ile-Ife, to participate in carefully chosen pieces for the musical concerts that have now become a regular fare at Trenchard Hall, and that draw full houses. To fill the lower and upper floors of Trenchard Hall as the musical concerts of recent years have done, means to bring together almost one thousand people to an evening performance. The audiences have always been a mixed grill of the old and middle-aged couples and younger people. Whilst the university staff and students constitute a good half of the audience, the university has been able to bring to Trenchard Hall from Ibadan city, the other half commute gladly to the university campus anytime a concert is announced.

The cultural rejuvenation of the university and town[27] community has been especially thrilling to such alumni as had witnessed a similar

---

27 Town and Gown.

bustle of activity and aesthetic delights in the 1950s, when the university was much smaller. To achieve a feat of similar impact at a time when competitive interests are greater in number, and when the economy is hasher, deserves commendation and a large portion of the praise goes to the Vice-Chancellor, Professor Ayo Banjo, who has created the atmosphere, physical, mental, aesthetic, and more importantly, financial, in which culture can be nourished. The impact has not only been felt at Trenchard Hall, but also at the Arts Theater that is now looking very attractive and that has become once again, a joy to perform or observe a performance. The Department of Theater Arts and the entire University of Ibadan community can look back on three years of resurgence and forward to many more years of similar growth with Christopher Oyesiku taking the firm roots.

The musical concert of Thursday, 30 March, 1989, scheduled to begin at half past seven, did not actually begin until quarter to eight due to *Nepatitis.*[28] This unusual lateness in beginning gave the latecomers (largely students who had been attending the 7:00 PM – 8:00 PM lectures), the opportunity to benefit from most of the evening's festivities. Christopher Oyesiku's concerts always show a sense of variety not only in selection but in genres. Vocal renditions are generally followed by piano recitals or other kinds of instrumental performances. The lights dimmed and comes up again is pianist, Godwin Sadoh, who rendered on piano with great talent and effectiveness three pieces: Chopin's "Valse" Op. 70, No. 2 in F minor, Mendelssohn's "Song Without Words, Op. 19, No. 3 in A Major," and the Ife based Joshua Uzoigwe's "Nigerian Dances No. 3." Godwin Sadoh deserves to be thanked both for his recital of Chopin and Mendelssohn and for drawing attention to the craft and talent of the Nigerian composer, Joshua Uzoigwe.

---

28 Dapo Adelugba lampoons the incessant electric power failure caused by NEPA— Nigerian Electric Power Authority.

**Christopher Oyesiku at the University of Ibadan
Commencement, 1995.**

The Yoruba have an apt saying, "Egun agba nii kehin igbale."[29] When veteran singer and choir-builder Christopher Oyesiku took the stage with his accompanist, Amorelle Inanga, it was clear to the audience that the evening was coming to an end. Before singing three songs in his rich bass voice, Christopher Oyesiku introduced the first of his three pieces: from Ponchielli's *La Gioconda*, he was to render *Scene ed Aria La Turbini*; thereafter, Michael Head's *Money, O!* And finally, Wilfred Sanderson's "Friend O' Mine." Christopher Oyesiku left the audience in no doubt about his mastery of the art and craft of singing, and Amorelle Inanga was as usual highly engaging on the piano. What he performed, he did with utmost skill and beauty, and the evening came to an impressive end when all the participants came on stage for the final bow, followed by hand shakes with Professor Ayo Banjo, the Vice-Chancellor and with Mrs. Alice Banjo. Christopher Oyesiku brought the attention of the audience to the announcement on the back of the program of the next concert scheduled for Sunday, 7 May, 1989, that would feature the University of Ibadan Choir in Bach's *Peasant Cantata*.

Much as the ongoing exhilaration of musical life at Ibadan deserves to be applauded, it should be pointed out that there is need here and elsewhere for a broadening of the base of our music concerts to include a wider choice of musical fare. The predominance of Bach, Mozart, Chopin, Mendelssohn, with a few folk tunes thrown in for good measure, should begin to give way to a more catholic fare of historically varied Euro-American, Latin American, Caribbean, Oriental, Australian, and African music of various genres. Even staying within the confines of twentieth century compositions, we can now speak of the early twentieth, mid-twentieth and late twentieth centuries' creativities with their different flavors and forms. Special attention should also be given to African music, folk, traditional and contemporary—vocal and instrumental.

---

29   Literally translates as "the best performance by the *maestro* is reserved for the end of the concert."

Then there is the all-important issue of continuity in tradition. We need to nourish a new generation of trained musicians and singers, preferably with a catholic taste in world music as well as a firm grasp of African traditions of music—folk, traditional, and contemporary. The universities have their role to play; in addition, there should be studios, arts centers, academies or institutes, and conservatories where the new generation could acquire a full training leading to professional expertise.

Christopher Oyesiku is a living example of professionalism. While we gladly gaze up at his six-foot figure in admiration and excitedly clap our hands after each performance in appreciation, we should be aware of the urgent necessity of producing a new generation of Oyesiku in singing and in all the other departments of the art of music-making. New virtuosos should also emerge in all the other creative arts. Thus, we would ensure that the music concerts and arts events of the twenty-first century would be even more satisfying for those coming hereafter than the twentieth century concerts at Ibadan and elsewhere have been for us.[30]

---

30 Professor Dapo Adelugba, "Tribute to A Virtuoso," *Daily Sketch,* Thursday, 20 April, 1989.

Epilogue

One of the salient features of Christopher Oyesiku's distinguished solo and choral career was his meticulous and innovative song repertoire that was always globally intercultural. His choice of songs ranged from European classical, to African-American spirituals, Latin-American, Caribbean, to indigenous Nigerian folk songs, and of course, modern Nigerian art songs such as Ayo Bankole's *Three Yoruba Songs.*[31] Oyesiku sang these songs in 2005 at a memorial concert in honor of Ayo Bankole's seventieth anniversary (1935-2005), organized by the Center for Intercultural Music Arts, at the University of Cambridge, London. The late Ayo Bankole dedicated most of his solo songs to Oyesiku whom he studied with at the Guildhall School of Music and Drama, London, and later, a colleague at the Nigerian Broadcasting Corporation, Lagos. At Oyesiku's concerts, he strove to satisfy the musical appetite of the Europeans, the average classical music oriented Nigerians and those itching for songs in Nigerian native languages, particularly the Yoruba. Oyesiku was well known in Nigeria, West Africa, and Great Britain as an extraordinary *basso profundo*.

Even though he has retired from active music career, Oyesiku's ingenuity lives on. His magnificent efforts have touched the lives of

---

31   Ayo Bankole, *Three Yoruba Songs* (Ile-Ife: University of Ife Press, 1976).

so many Nigerians including his colleagues and more importantly, the younger generation that would carry-on the baton from where he stopped. The process to sought after those who would fit into Oyesiku's shoes might appears to be a 'mission impossible;' but, may I point out that Oyesiku has impacted and influenced several younger, budding, and talented musicians in Nigeria; thereby, challenging them to maintain the course, step up the standard, and fudge ahead into new vistas of musical creativity and performance. Therefore, we should not be surprised to observe not too far in the nearest future, a new crop of the Oyesiku's *basso profundo* and indefatigable classical concertmasters all over Nigeria.

Concert Programs

WAREHAM CHURCH
FRIDAY, DECEMBER 7TH, 1956
7.45 P.M.

Member Choirs :

Bryantspuddle Singers   Puddletown Singers
Isle of Purbeck Arts Club   Winfrith Choral Society
Wool Singers

SHERBORNE ABBEY
SATURDAY, DECEMBER 8TH
7.45 P.M.

Member Choirs :

Alton Pancras Singers   Evershot Singers
Corfe Mullen Choral Society   Isle of Purbeck Arts Club
Donhead Choral Society   Silton Singers
Wimborne Choral Society

Conductor	... ...	PAUL STEINITZ
Soprano	... ...	NOELLE BARKER
Contralto	... ...	DELIA WOOLFORD
Tenor	... ...	EDGAR FLEET
Bass	... ...	CHRISTOPHER OYESIKU

BACH CANTATA CLUB ORCHESTRA

Guest Leader	...	REGINALD MORLEY
Organ	... ...	JOHN DUSSEK

PROGRAMME (Performer)

Copies of the words will be available at the performance

Dorset Guild of Singers Performing J. S. Bach *Three Cantatas*, 1956.

89

THE
UNITED HOSPITALS'
CHOIR

Conductor: - BUXTON ORR

Organ: - JOHN CLARK

VALERIE CARDNELL	JANET COSTER
Soprano	*Contralto*
WILLIAM MACE	CHRISTOPHER OYESIKU
Tenor	*Bass*

THURSDAY, 4th APRIL, 1957

at 8.30 p.m.

Church of St. George-the-Martyr,
Queen Square.

Admission by Programme : 3/6

**The United Hospitals Choir Concert at
Church of Saint George-the-Martyr, 1957.**

DER FREISCHUTZ

A romantic opera first produced in Berlin in 1821

Libretto by Friedrich Kind   *Music by Weber*
English Translation by Natalia MacFarren

CHARACTERS IN ORDER OF APPEARANCE

MAX, *a forester*.	*Barry Harries
	†Edgar Thomas
KILIAN, *a peasant*	*John Down
	†Gordon Willis
CUNO, *head-ranger*	David Lewis
CASPAR, *a forester*	*Russell Smith
	†Delme Jones
ANNIE, *neice to Cuno*	*Janet Young
	†Joan Passmore
AGATHE, *Cuno's daughter – betrothed to Max*	*Lorna Elias
	†Mary Bass
ZAMIEL, *the Black Huntsman*	*Delme Jones
	†Russell Smith
AN APPARITION	Sandra Griffith
FIRST BRIDESMAID	Margaret Rees
SECOND BRIDESMAID	Phyllis Glavin
THIRD BRIDESMAID	Mary Eley
FOURTH BRIDESMAID	Margaret Whittle
PRINCE OTTOKAR	Benjamin Luxon
THE HERMIT	*Christopher Oyesiku
	†Michael Tooby

CHORUS OF VILLAGERS AND FORESTERS: Jessica Bonar, Corrine Bridge, Mary Eley, Gloria Farndell, Phyllis Glavin, Gillian Goodwin, Joan Lock, Margaret Rees, Rosemary Scott, Margaret Whittle, Colin Atkin, David Bacon, William Cheffers, Peter Collier, John Down, John Major, Roy Murray, David Rayson, Ramon Remedios, Harry Rolfe, Gordon Willis.

* *Tuesday and Friday.* † *Wednesday, Thursday and Saturday.*

The scene is laid in the Bohemian Forest
ACT I: An open space in the Forest
ACT II Scene 1: A room in the Head-Ranger's Lodge
Scene 2: The Wolf's Glen
ACT III Scene 1: Same as ACT I Scene 2 next morning
Scene 2: Same as ACT I Scene 1 later that day

There will be an interval of fifteen minutes between Acts II and III during which refreshments may be obtained

Guildhall School of Music and Drama Performing Weber's *Der Freischutz*, 1960.

SONATA IN D MAJOR OPUS. 1 No. 13   HANDEL

FOR VIOLIN AND KEYBOARD

Handel is belatedly coming to be recognised as one of the greatest melodists ever to have lived. German by birth, Italian by temperament and inclination and English by adoption, he conquered the musical public wherever he went and it is not hard to see why. He added little to the musical language of his day but took the style and forms which he found established in Italy, the centre of the musical world in that period and infused them with his distinctive grandeur and melody. Beethoven said of Handel "Go and learn of him how to achieve great effects with simple means." In his violin sonatas the form and language are those of Corelli, the originator of the Italian solo violin sonata, but the voice is unmistakably that of Handel whose forthright tunefulness makes all four movements memorable.

DOREEN BUSBRIDGE   ANN BUCHANAN
(VIOLIN)   (PIANO)

ARIA: O TU PALERMO   VERDI.
(THE SICILIAN VESPERS)

The opera—The Sicilian Vespers deals with the massacre of the French occupying army of Sicily at Palermo on Easter Monday 1282. Giovanni Di Procida, exiled by the French, returns secretly to the land of his birth. His aria tells of the joy at once more treading his native soil and his desire to rouse his country-men to throw off the invaders' yoke.

WE KNOW NO THOUGHT OF VENGEANCE   MOZART.
(MAGIC FLUTE)

This is the second of the two great arias which are sung in the opera by Sarastro, the High Priest. It comes in the second act. Pamina was ordered to kill Sarastro by her mother the Queen of Night. They were overheard by Monostatos an evil slave, who threatens to reveal the plot to Sarastro unless Pamina submits to his passion. Sarastro enters just in time to save Pamina and reveals that he knows about her mother's evil intentions. Pamina pleads for her mother and Sarastro replies with this exposition of the creed of Isis—We know no thought of vengeance within these temple walls.

VERRAT. (TREACHERY)   BRAHMS.

As I lingered by my sweetheart's door I saw it open and a man steps out. She whispered to him "My lover is far away, come to me again tomorrow". You had better hasten, my dainty thief! A man is waiting for you out on the moor; and morning's light will show a dead man in the heather!

SEA FEVER   JOHN IRELAND.

The words of this stirring song are by the English Poet Laureate, John Masefield.

"I must go down to the sea again.
To the lonely sea and the sky".

This is a fine song in which both the words and the music are perfectly wedded together.

JA ITANNA TO NTAN.   AYO BANKOLE

This song was written by request and it represents the composer's idea of the adaptation of some of the international technique in harmony and composition to enrich a background which is essentially Nigerian. "Ja itanna to ntan" illustrates the theme "Never leave until the morrow the good that can be done today". An interesting feature in this song is the subtle manner in which the ticking of the clock is introduced and depicted.

CHRISTOPHER OYESIKU   ANN BUCHANAN
(BASS)   (ACCOMPANIST)

SONATA IN D MAJOR }   SCARLATTI
SONATA IN D MINOR }

Born in 1685, a year to be remembered by all music lovers as it also saw the birth of Handel and Bach, Scarlatti wrote a great number of keyboard sonatas, most of them gay little pieces, full of high spirits. Such is the first of these two, while the second is quieter, with a flowing "Pastorale" rhythm popular in Scarlatti's day.

IMPROMPTU IN E FLAT, OPUS 90 No. 2   SCHUBERT.

This Impromptu, one of a set of eight, has all the youthful drive and vigour we associate with Schubert's early creative years, when he poured out music at an astonishing rate, even producing sometimes in one day's work several songs and some instrumental music.

MALAGUENA   }   ALBENIZ
SEGUIDILLAS }

Albeniz, born in Spain in 1860, was a child prodigy who had given piano recitals in many countries before he was 14. When later, he turned to composition, he used in most of his piano music the traditional Spanish dance rhythm, often suggesting also the characteristic guitar playing and vocal styles of various parts of the country.

MARGARET EVANS

Boy Scouts Association of Nigeria Concert of International Classical Music, 1962.

PROGRAMME

1. PRO MUSICA LAGOS

Trio Sonata in C Major, for Recorder, Flute, and Basso Continuo — Johann Joachim Quantz

Affettuoso
Alla Breve
Larghetto
Vivace

Trio Sonata in F Major, for Recorder, Bassoon, and Basso Continuo — George Fhilipp Telemann

Vivace
Mesto
Allegro

Brook Byron—*Flute*, Franz Nagel—*Recorder*, Sarah Garrison—*Violoncello*
Stephen Perritt—*Bassoon*, Kenneth Jones—*Harpsichord*.

2. SONGS

Recit: I Rage, I Rage
Aria: O Ruddier Then The Cherry (Acis and Galatea) — Handel
Recit: Frondi Tenere
Aria: Ombra Mai Fu — Handel
    (Serse)
The Song of Momus to Mars — Boyce
O Hear Us Isis and Osiris — Mozart
    (The Magic Flute)

Christopher Oyesiku — *Bass*
Akin Euba — *Accompanist*

3. PIANO SOLOS

Intermezzo in A Minor — Brahms
Rhapsody in D Minor — Brahms

Robin Briars

INTERVAL

4. SONGS

When a Maiden Takes Your Fancy — Mozart
(Il Seraglio)
Il Lacerato Spirito — Verdi
(Simon Boccanegra)
La Turbini E Farnetichi — Ponchielli
(La Gioconda)

Christopher Oyesiku — *Bass*
Akin Euba — *Accompanist*

5. PRO MUSICA LAGOS

Concerto a tre, for Recorder, Bassoon, and Basso Continuo — George Philipp Telemann
Allegro moderato
Loure
Tempo di Menuet

Sonata in D Major, for Flute, Violoncello, and Harpsichord
Allegro con spirito
Andante
Rondo Scherzo

Brook Byron—*Flute*, Franz Nagel—*Recorder*, Sarah Garrison—*Violoncello*
Stephen Perritt—*Bassoon*, Kenneth Jones—*Harpsichord*

6. PIANO SOLOS

Ballade in Ab Major, — Chopin
Nocturne in Ab Major, — Liszt

Robin Briars

7. SONGS

In Summertime on Bredon — Graham Peel
Simon the Cellarer — Hatton
Sea Fever — John Ireland
Kiniun — Ayo Bankole
Iya — Ayo Bankole

Christopher Oyesiku — *Bass*
Akin Euba — *Accompanist*

DURING THE INTERVAL DRINKS WILL BE AVAILABLE AT THE BAR.

The British High Commissioner After Dinner Concert, Lagos, 1966.

Lagos Musical Society Choir

and

Christ Church Cathedral Choir

present

A Concert of Christmas Music

at the

Cathedral Church of Christ, Lagos.

Conductor: Christopher Oyesiku

Friday 16th December, 1966 at 9.00 p.m.

Cecilia Odiah

Christina Le Moignan

Harold Potts

Brian Harvey

Trumpeters of the Central Band of the Nigeria Police

Organ: Obayomi Phillips

Lagos Musical Society Choir and Cathedral Church of Christ Choir at a Concert of Christmas Music, 1966.

CHRISTOPHER OYESIKU BASS SINGER

AYO BANKOLE PIANIST and COMPOSER

Two Nigerian Artists of high reputation in West Africa in a

CLASSICAL CONCERT

comprising works by Handel, Mozart, Schubert, Brahms, Verdi and Ayo Bankole on Wednesday, May 3rd 1967, at 8.00 p.m. at the Arts Centre 28th February Road, Accra.

Admission: N¢0.50 and N¢0.25

Advance booking advisable: Arts Centre or Goethe Institute

PROGRAMME

I feel, I feel — Georg Friedrich Handel
Arm, Arm, Ye Brave
(Judas Macabaeus)
Si tra I Ceppi — Georg Friedrich Handel
Now Phoebus sinketh in the West — Thomas Arne
O hear us Isis and Osiris — Wolfgang A. Mozart
(Zauberflote)
Variations on: Ah, vous dirai-je — Wolfgang A. Mozart
Marnam — Franz Schubert
Aufenthalt — Hugo Wolf
Verborgenheit — Johannes Brahms
Verni

INTERVAL

When a Ma den takes your Fancy — Wolfgang A. Mozart
(Il Seraglio)
O tu Palermo — Giuseppe Verdi
(I vespri Siciliani)
Variations Liturgic — Ayo Bankole
In Summertime on Bredon — Graham Peel
Captain Stratton's Fancy — Peter Warlock
Shorting Bread — Jaques Wolfe
Adura Mi — Ayo Bankole
Kinium — Ayo Bankole
Ja Itan To Nian — Ayo Bankole

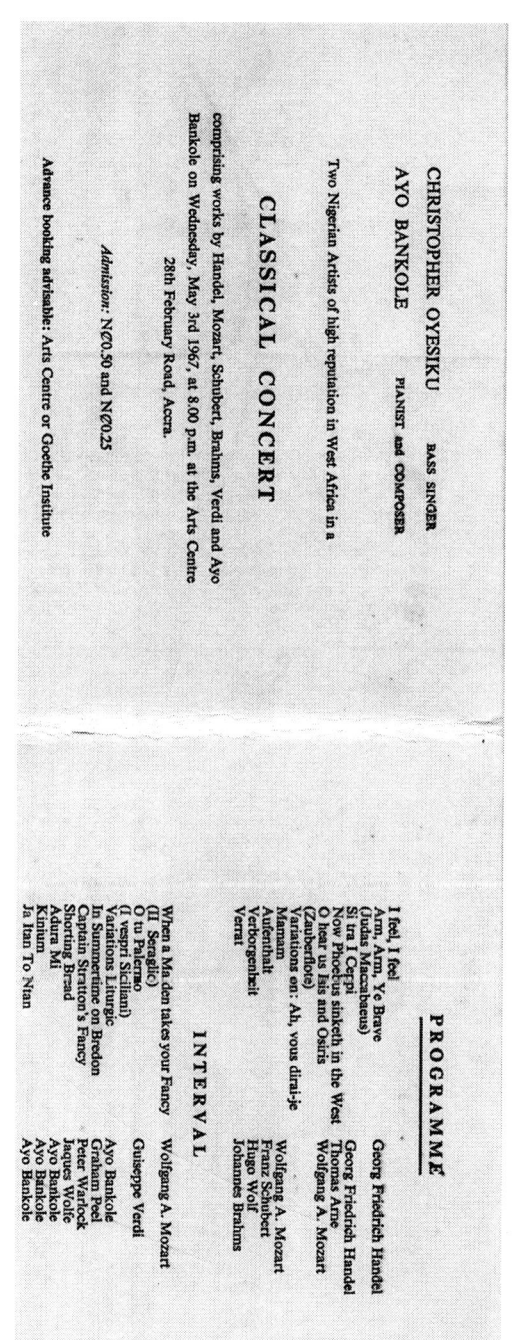

Christopher Oyesiku and Ayo Bankole at the Department of Art
and Culture and the Goethe Institute, 1967.

UNIVERSITY OF IBADAN MUSIC CIRCLE

8 and 9 MAY 1970

GEORGE FREDERICK HANDEL

Acis and Galatea

A SERENATA

Composed about the Year 1720

Part One

WE ARE in the land of the ancient Immortals, so beloved of eighteenth-century poets. Happy nymphs and swains dance and sport the hours away. Amid such ideal surroundings Galatea alone is restless, and begs the birds to hush their singing and bring back her beloved Acis.

Acis enters and, guided by Damon, finds his beloved and calls to her: "Love in her eyes sits playing". After Galatea's reply—"As when the dove laments her love"—the two join in a duet of happiness, echoed later by the Chorus.

But alas, "Wretched lovers, quit your dream. Fate has passed this sad decree: No joy shall last." Behold the monster Polypheme, at whose coming the whole world trembles. The giant, demanding a huge pipe for his capacious mouth wherewith to make music, serenades the horrified Galatea with absurd flatteries: "O ruddier than the cherry, O sweeter than the berry, O nymph more bright than moonshine night, like kidlings blithe and merry". Damon, adviser to everybody, tries to restrain the monster's clumsiness, but Acis rises up in gallant anger—"Love sounds the alarm, and fear is a-flying!" Galatea tries to calm him, and together they profess the constancy of their love, but it is too late: the Polypheme strikes Acis with a mortal blow.

There is great lamenting. The gentle Acis is no more, and Galatea is grief-stricken. But the Chorus begs her to make use of her divine powers: she cannot bring Acis back to life but she can give him immortality by transforming him into a river: "To kindred gods the youth return, through verdant plains to roll his urn". No sooner said than done: "Be thou immortal, though thou art not mine!"—and she sits peacefully by the stream as it "murmurs still his gentle love". The Chorus has the last word:

> Galatea, dry thy tears:
> Acis now a god appears.
> See how he rears him from his bed,
> See the wreath that binds his head!
> Hail! thou gentle murmuring stream,
> Shepherds' pleasure, muses' theme,
> Through the plains still joy to rove,
> Murmuring still thy gentle love.

Galatea	Joan Cooray
Acis	'Şina Ojęmuyiwa
Polypheme	Christopher Oyesiku '.
Damon	Robert Home

Chorus of Nymphs and Shepherds: The Choirs of the Music Circle and of the International School.

Acis and Galatea Serenata by the University of Ibadan Music Circle, 1970.

CATHEDRAL CHURCH OF CHRIST
LAGOS

THE L.M.S. and N.B.C. CHOIRS

Concert of Christmas Music

Soloist

JOAN COORAY	—	*Soprano*
CHRISTOPHER OYESIKU	—	*Conductor*
OBAYOMI PHILLIPS	—	*Organ*

Trumpeters of the Central Band of the
Nigeria Police

The Lagos Musical Society Concert of Christmas Music, 1971.

Officiating Ministers

The Right Revd. S. I. KALE, *D.D.*
Bishop of Lagos

The Revd. Prof. BOLAJI IDOWU, *Ph.D.*
President of the Methodist Church of Nigeria

The Very Revd. SOPE JOHNSON, B.D.
Provost, Cathedral Church of Christ, Lagos

With the

LAGOS MUSICAL SOCIETY CHOIR

Directed by

CHRISTOPHER OYESIKU

ORGAN: **KAYODE ONI,** *F.T.C.L., A.R.C.M., A.L.C.M., L.T.C.L.*

ORGANIST: **C. B. OGUNDEJI**

VICAR: **The Revd. D. O. ONI**

Wedding Service of Olatokunbo Ayoka Awolowo and Gbolahan Olusiji Dosumu at Saint Savior's Anglican Church, Ikenne, 1973.

The Nigerian Broadcasting Corporation

Festival of
Nine Lessons and Carols

by the

N. B. C. CHOIR

at

St. Peter's Church, Faji, Lagos

Saturday, 24th December, 1977
at 8.30 p.m.

The Nigerian Broadcasting Corporation Choir Festival of Nine
Lessons and Carols at Saint Peter's Anglican Church, Lagos, 1977.

Federal Radio Corporation of Nigeria
Lagos

Festival of
Nine Lessons and Carols

by the

F. R. C. N. CHOIR

St. Peter's Church, Faji, Lagos

Monday, 24th December, 1979
at 8.30 p.m.

The Nigerian Broadcasting Corporation Choir Festival of Nine
Lessons and Carols at Saint Peter's Anglican Church, Lagos, 1979.

100

SERVICE SUNG

AT THE REQUEST OF

SAINT PAUL'S (BREADFRUIT) PROGRESSIVES

BY THE

RADIO NIGERIA CHOIR, LAGOS

DIRECTED BY

CHRISTOPHER OYESIKU

WITH

KAYODE ONI

AT THE

ORGAN

OFFICIATING PRIEST

THE VEN. ARCHDEACON B. A. ADELAJA, M.A., D.TH.
Vicar of Saint Paul's Church (Breadfruit)
and
Archdeacon of Lagos

**Radio Nigeria Choir in Choral Evensong at
Saint Paul's Anglican Church, Breadfruit, Lagos, 1981.**

PROGRAMME

Ave Maria — Bach-Gounod
Bless This House — Brahe
Adura Fun Alafia — Ayo Bankole

Funmi Akinkugbe — Soprano
Tolu Obajimi — Accompanist

Sonata In C   K. 330 — Mozart
Allegro Moderato
Andante Cantabile
Allegretto

Joyce Lowe — Piano

Serenade (Berceuse) — Gounod
Nacht Und Traume — Schubert
Printemps Qui Commence — Saint-Saens
(Samson Et Dalila)
Mo R'oko R'oko — Kehinde Okusanya
Tuzu — Joshua Uzoigwe

Mosunmola Omibiyi-Obidike — Mezzo Soprano
Thora duBois — Accompanist

Nocturne In F Sharp Major — Chopin
OP. 15. No 2.
Waltz In G Flat Major — Chopin
OP. 70 No 1.

Thora duBois — Piano

INTERVAL 15 MINUTES

Art Thou Troubled (Rodelinda) — Handel
Ombra Mai Fu (Serse) — Handel
Adura Mi — Ayo Bankole
Ojo Ma Ro — Ayo Bankole

Femi Akinkugbe — Soprano
Tolu Obajimi — Accompanist

Variations Serieuses In D Minor. OP. 54 — Mendelssohn

Thora duBois — Piano

Recit: O Patria
Aria: O Tu Palermo (I Vespri Siciliani) — Verdi

Verrat — Brahms
Sea Fever — John Ireland
Simon the Cellarer — John Hatton

Christopher Oyesiku — Bass
Thora duBois — Accompanist

The University of Ibadan, Department of Theater Arts Concert,
March 1988.

102

PROGRAMME

Si, Tra i Ceppi (Berenice) — Handel

In Diesen Heil'gen Hallen (Die Zauberflote) — Mozart

Christopher Oyesiku — Bass
Obayomi Phillips — Accompanist

Prelude In E Major — J. S. Bach
Corrente From Partita. V. — J. S. Bach
Finale From Sonata. Op. 17. No. 2. — J. C. Bach
Sonata In G Major — Haydn
Allegro Con Brio
Menuetto
Trio
Rondo.

Gbenga Kayode-Smith — Piano

Victorious My Heart Is — Carissimi
O Del Mio Dolce Ardor (Faride Ed Elena) — Gluck

Moon River — Mauchini

Eriri Ngeringe — Joshua Uzoigwe
Uyaroma — Joshua Uzoigwe
Tuzu — Joshua Uzoigwe

Joyce Adewumi — Soprano
Joshua Uzoigwe — Accompanist

The Judge's Song (Trial By Jury) — Sullivan
The Pirate King's Song (The Pirate of Penzance) — Sullivan
I am The Very Model of a Modern Major General (The Pirate of Penzance) — Sullivan
My Boy You May Take It From Me (Ruddigore) — Sullivan

When The Night Wind Howls (Ruddigore) — Sullivan
The Mikado's Song (The Mikado) — Sullivan

Michael Hudson — Baritone
Joyce Lowe — Accompanist

INTERVAL 15 MINUTES

In These Delightful, Pleasant Groves — Purcell
Sweet and Low — Barnby
Love Fare Thee Well — Brahms
The Blue Danube — Johann Strauss
Arranged for S.A.T.B.
By: Arthur Pearson

E Je K'a Sise O — Dayo Dedeke
Iwe Kiko — Dayo Dedeke

THE CHOIR OF THE UNIVERSITY OF IBADAN
Christopher Oyesiku — Conductor
Emmanuel Boamah — Accompanist

Sonata No 14 In C Sharp Minor Op. 27 No. 2. (Moonlight) — Beethoven
Adagio Sostenuto
Allegretto
Presto Agitato

Amorelle Inanga — Piano

Say Goodbye Now to Pastime And Play, Lad (The Marriage of Figaro) — Mozart
Linden Lea — Vaughan Williams
Iya — Ayo Bankole

Christopher Oyesiku — Bass
Obayomi Phillips — Accompanist

The University of Ibadan, Department of Theater Arts Silver Jubilee Concert, July 1988.

103

PROGRAMME

Arise, Ye Subterranean Winds
(Tempest) — Purcell

Recit: Frondi Tenere
Aria: Ombra Mai Fu
(Serse) — Handel

The Song of Momus to Mars — Boyce

In Diesen Heil'gen Hallen
(Die Zauberflöte) — Mozart

Christopher Oyesiku - Bass
Amorelle Inanga - Accompanist

Sonata in C. K. 330 — Mozart
Allegro Moderato
Andante Cantabile
Allegretto

Joyce Lowe - Piano

The Judge's Song
(Trial by Jury) — Sullivan

The First Lord's Song
(H.M.S. Pinafore) — Sullivan

The Pirate King's Song
(The Pirate of Penzance) — Sullivan

The Mikado's Song
(The Mikado) — Sullivan

Michael Hudson - Baritone
Joyce Lowe - Accompanist

Nocturne Op.55 No1. in F Minor — Chopin
Arabesque No1. in E Major — Debussy
Nigerian Dances No 3. — Joshua Uzoigwe

Godwin Sadoh - Piano

INTERVAL 20 MINUTES

Sonata in C Sharp Minor
'Moonlight' Op.27 No 2. — Beethoven
Adagio Sostenuto
Allegretto
Presto Agitato

Amorelle Inanga - Piano

Scena E Romanza
IL Lacerato Spirito
(Simon Boccanegra) — Verdi

In Summertime on Bredon — Graham Peel
Iya — Ayo Bankole
Ja Itanna To Ntan — Ayo Bankole
Short'nin Bread — Jacques Wolfe

Christopher Oyesiku - Bass
Amorelle Inanga - Accompanist

Farewell Concert for Dr. Natalie Hahn at the International Institute of Tropical Agriculture, Ibadan, 1989.

104

UNIVERSITY OF IBADAN

DEPARTMENT OF THEATRE ARTS

Presents a

IN THE PRESENCE OF

PROFESSOR AYO BANJO PH.D.
THE VICE-CHANCELLOR

and

MRS ALICE BANJO

SPECIAL GUESTS

CHIEF & MRS. OLAYIWOLA BALOGUN

MR. & MRS. RAYMOND ZARD

TRENCHARD HALL
SUNDAY, 2ND SEPTEMBER 1990
AT 7.30 P.M.

PROFESSOR FEMI OSOFISAN HEAD OF THE DEPARTMENT OF THEATRE ARTS U. I.	**CHRISTOPHER OYESIKU** ARTISTE-IN-RESIDENCE U. I.

The University of Ibadan, Department of Theater Arts Concert,
July 1990.

PROGRAMME

University Anthem — Words by Professor Isidore Okpewho / Music by Olaolu Omideyi

In these Delightful Pleasant Groves — Purcell
The Lass with the Delicate Air — Michael Arne / Arranged for S.A.T.B. by John West

Non Nobis, Domine — Roger Quilter

University of Ibadan Choir
Christopher Oyesiku—Conductor
Emmanuel Boamah—Accompanist

Voi Che Sapete--Ye Who Have Duly Learnt Cupid's Art (The Marriage of Figaro) — Mozart
The Trout — Schubert
Mo Le Jiyan Yo — Akin Euba
Ore-Meta — Akin Euba

Sade Ogunsola—Soprano
Tolu Obajimi—Accompanist

Fantasie in C Minor KV 975 — Mozart
Adagio
Allegro
Andantino
Piu Allegro
Adagio

Willem Platteeuw—Piano

Recit: Perfidi — Verdi
Aria: Pieta, Rispetto Amore (Macbeth)
Aria: Pescator Affonda L'esca (La Gioconda) — Ponchielli
My Name is John Wellington Wells (The Sorcerer) — Sullivan
Recit: Am I Alone, and Unobserved? — Sullivan
Aria: If You're Anxious for to Shine (Patience)

INTERVAL 15 MINUTES

Scherzo in B Flat — Schubert
Impromptu in E — Franz Liszt
Theme and Variations on a Traditional Tune -- Maye Kom — Emmanuel Boamah

Emmanuel Boamah—Piano

Lord God of Abraham (Elijah) — Mendelssohn
Deh Vieni Alla Finestra (Don Giovanni) — Mozart
When the Nightwind Howls (Ruddigore) — Sullivan

David Williams—Baritone
Amorelle Inanga—Accompanist

Miniatures — Frank Bridge
Minuet
Gavotte
Allegretto

Galiya Ogunlesi—Violin
Glen Inanga—Violoncello
Amorelle Inanga—Piano

Far Away — Harmonized and Arranged by James Mansfield
The Blue Danube — Johann Strauss / Arranged for S.A.T.B. by Arthur Pearson
Steal Away — Fela Sowande
My Way's Cloudy — Fela Sowande

The University of Ibadan Choir
Christopher Oyesiku—Conductor
Emmanuel Boamah—Accompanist

* Theme by Elsie Izola

The University of Ibadan, Department of Theater Arts
End of Session Concert, July 1991.

Se Vuol Ballare	Mozart
(The Marriage of Figaro)	
Hor Ich Das Liedchen Klingen	Schubert
Am Leuchtenden Sommermorgen	
(Dichterliebe)	
The Hippopotamus	Swann
(At the Drop of a Hat)	

David Williams--Baritone
Amorelle Inanga--Accompanist

Sonata No. 15 in C Major K545	Mozart
Allegro	
Andante	
Rondo--Allegretto Grazioso	
Ya Orule	Ayo Bankole
Variations on a Theme for Little Ayo	Ayo Bankole

Ayo Bankole Jr.--Piano

Recit: I Rage, I Rage	Handel
Aria: O Ruddier than the Cherry	
(Acis and Galatea)	
Recit: A te L'Estremo Addio	Verdi
Aria: Il Lacerato Spirito	
(Simon Boccanegra)	
Friend O' Mine	Wilfrid Sanderson
Short'nin Bread	Jacques Wolfe

Christopher Oyesiku--Bass
Emmanuel Boamah--Accompanist

♫ ♪ *Thank You for Coming* ♪ ♫

The Music Circle, University of Ibadan,
Birthday Celebration Concert, 1991.

PROGRAMME

University Anthem — Words by Professor Isidore Okpewho / Music by Olaolu Omideyi

The Lass with the Delicate Air — Michael Arne / *Arranged for SATB by John West*

Breathe Soft, Ye Winds — William Paxton

When My Lady Walks in Beauty — William Rains

University of Ibadan Choir
Christopher Oyesiku – Conductor
Adeniran Obasa – Piano

Sonata in F Major KV 332 — Amadeus Mozart
Allegro
Adagio
Assai Allegro

Willem Platteeuw – Piano

Aria: Pescator Affonda L'esca (La Gioconda) — Amilcare Ponchielli

My Name is John Wellington Wells (The Sorcerer) — Arthur Sullivan

Recit: Am I Alone and Unobserved?
Aria: If You Are Anxious for to Shine (Patience) — Arthur Sullivan

Michael Hudson – Baritone
Joyce Lowe – Piano

Sonata in C Minor — Jean-Baptiste Loeillet
Adagio
Allegro
Gavotte
Sarabande – Lento
Gigue – Vivace

Zeal Onyia – Trumpet

INTERVAL – 15 MINUTES

Recit: The Star that Bids the Shepherd Fold
Aria: Now Phoebus Sinketh in the West — Thomas Arne

Verrat — Johannes Brahms

Simon the Cellarer — John Hatton

Christopher Oyesiku – Bass
Amorelle Inanga – Piano

Sonata in G Minor — Attilio Ariosti
Andante
Allegro
Andante
Allegro

Ajibola Meshida – Violin
Richard Bucknor – Piano

Tom Ploughboy — Leonard Horton
Love, Fare Thee Well — Johannes Brahms
Linden Lea — Vaughan Williams / *Arranged for SATB by Arthur Somervell*
Wein, Weib und Gesang Op. 333 — Johann Strauss (Jnr) / *Arranged for SATB by Henry Gheel*

University of Ibadan Choir
Christopher Oyesiku – Conductor
Adeniran Obasa – Piano

Forthcoming Event
Music Circle
Nigeria Independence Anniversary Concert
Friday 2nd October 1992
in the Trenchard Hall

The University of Ibadan, Department of Theater Arts
End of Session Concert, July 1992.

Eine Kleine Nachtmusik K.525·		Mozart
Allegro		
Andante		
Allegretto		
	Galiya Ogunlesi — Violin	
	Amorelle Inanga — Piano	

When I, Good Friends, Was Called To The Bar		Sullivan
(Trial By Jury)		
When I Was a Lad		Sullivan
(H.M.S. Pinafore)		
When All Night Long		Sullivan
(Iolanthe)		
The Mikado's Song		Sullivan
(The Mikado)		
	Michael Hudson — Baritone	
	Joyce Lowe — Piano	

Verrat		Brahms
The Old Superb		Stanford
Who'll Be A Witness		Fela Sowande
	Christopher Oyesiku — Bass	
	Amorelle Inanga — Piano	

The Moon Has Raised Her Lamp Above		Benedict
		Arranged for
		SATB by Noel Hannerford
Oh! Dear! What Can The Matter Be?		*Arranged by Alec Rowley*
Roll The Ol' Chariot		Fela Sowande
Salve Christe		Ayo Bankole
Funmi N'Ibeji		Ayo Bankole
Ojo Maro		Ayo Bankole
	University of Ibadan Choir	
	Christopher Oyesiku — Conductor	
	Christopher Ayodele — Piano	

Flowers by Elaine Jegede

The University of Ibadan, Department of Theater Arts 44th Anniversary Concert, 1992.

University of Ibadan
Department of Theatre Arts

Presents a

CONCERT

In the Presence of

Professor A.B.O.O. Oyediran, M.D.
Vice-Chancellor
University of Ibadan
and
Chief (Mrs.) Omotola Oyediran

Sponsor
and
Special Guest

Dr. Raymond Zard

Trenchard Hall of the University
Wednesday, 26th April 1995 at 7.30 P.M.

Professor Dapo Adelugba   Christopher Oyesiku
Head, Dept of Theatre Arts   Artiste-in-Residence

**The University of Ibadan, Department of Theater Arts Concert,
July 1995.**

P R O G R A M M E

Recit: I Feel the Deity Within
Aria: Arm, Arm Ye Brave — Handel
(Judas Maccabaeus)
Bois Epais (Sombre Woods) — Lully
Verrat (Treachery) — Brahms

Christopher Oyesiku — Bass
Christopher Ayodele — Piano

Sonata in A Minor — Attilio Ariosti
Adagio
Allegro
Andante
Allegro

Ajibola Meshida — Violin
Richard Bucknor — Piano

Ave Maria — Bach-Gounod
Vaghissima Sembianza — S. Donaudy
The Lass with a Delicate Air — Michael Arne
Nwoyoyo (Lullaby) — Laz Ekwueme

Laz Ekwueme — Tenor
Richard Bucknor — Piano

Sonata No. 14 in C Sharp Minor — Beethoven
Op. 27 No. 2 (*Moonlight*)
Adagio Sostenuto
Allegretto
Presto Agitato

Edward Boamah — Piano

INTERVAL — 15 MINUTES

Aria: Let the Bright Seraphim — Handel
(Samson)
Aria: Ah! Je Veux Vivre — Gounod
(Romeo et Juliette)
Oji Meme Onu — O'ndu Ndubuisi

Funmilayo Boamah — Soprano
Edward Boamah — Piano

Sonata in G Minor — Purcell
Largo
Allegro
Andante
Allegro

Ajibola Meshida — Violin
Richard Bucknor — Piano

Impromptu in E Flat Major No. 2 — Schubert
Prelude in C Sharp Minor Op. 3 No 2 — Rachmaninov

Edward Boamah — Piano

Aria: Say Goodbye Now to
Pastime and Play, Lad — Mozart
(The Marriage of Figaro)
Scena E Romanza — Verdi
Il Lacerato Spirito
(Simon Boccanegra)
Ja Itanna to Ntan — Ayo Bankole
Song of the Flea — Moussorgsky
Arranged by Rimsky-Korsakov

Christopher Oyesiku — Bass
Christopher Ayodele — Piano

The University of Ibadan, Department of Theater Arts Concert, July 1995.

The Glory of Christmas Concert

List of Artistes

Funmilayo Boamah	* Soprano
Edward Boamah	* Piano
Richard Bucknor	* Piano
Niran Obasa	* Accompanist
Mosunmola Omibiyi-Obidike	* Mezzo-Soprano
Sina Ojemuyiwa	* Tenor
Gbenga Oyesanya	* Accompanist

The University of Ibadan Choir
Christopher Oyesiku, Conductor

**The Glory of Christmas Concert by the Music Circle,
University of Ibadan, 1996.**

Other Books by Godwin Sadoh

Thomas Ekundayo Phillips: The Doyen of Nigerian Church Music

Samuel Akpabot: The Odyssey of a Nigerian Composer-Ethnomusicologist

The Organ Works of Fela Sowande: Cultural Perspectives

Intercultural Dimensions in Ayo Bankole's Music

Joshua Uzoigwe: Memoirs of a Nigerian Composer-Ethnomusicologist

The Organ Works of Fela Sowande: A Nigerian Organist-Composer

Lightning Source UK Ltd.
Milton Keynes UK
UKOW04f0029281114

242327UK00001B/152/P